BREAK THE RULES
IN SELLING

Also by Michael Beer and published by Mercury Books:

The Joy of Selling
The Joy of Winning
Lead to Succeed
Diary of a Sales Manager

BREAK THE RULES IN SELLING

A manual for the *advanced* salesperson

Michael Beer

MERCURY

First published in 1991
by Mercury Books
Gold Arrow Publications Limited, 862 Garratt Lane, London SW17 0NB

Set in 11/12pt Plantin by TecSet Limited, Wallington, Surrey
Printed and bound in Great Britain by Mackays of Chatham, PLC, Chatham, Kent

British Library Cataloguing in Publication Data
Beer, Michael
  Break the rules in selling
  I. Title
  658.85

  ISBN 1-85252-078-7

CONTENTS

INTRODUCTION – THE ADVANCED SALESPERSON

You are an advanced salesperson.

You have been all the way there and all the way back again. You have walked the streets, driven the cars, knocked on the doors, made the phone calls, talked to the secretaries, arranged the interviews, shaken the hands, done the presentations, answered the questions, handled the objections and written the orders.

You have met with courtesy, rudeness, misunderstanding, complaints, apathy and congratulations.

You have sweated in summer and frozen in winter.

You have sweet-talked receptionists and cajoled traffic wardens.

You have known dressings-down from your manager, envy from your colleagues, impatience from your spouse. You have gloried in the joy of the enormous order and wallowed in the misery of the important lost sale.

You are an advanced salesperson.

If you were asked: 'What hundred things would you like to have at this moment?' I suppose that another book on selling would not be very high on your list; chances are it wouldn't appear at all.

This is another book on selling.

As I say, you are an advanced salesperson. So am I. I also happen to be a sales trainer, but that doesn't mean that I don't still have to sell. I sell training and if I don't sell it I don't eat, so in fact I am a commission salesman, in that I don't get a fixed salary. I am an advanced salesman. I have been where you have been. I have sold babies' bottles to pharmacies, bulldozers to government bodies, axle grease to trucking companies, annuities to pensioners, scissors to barbers, screwdrivers to hardware stores and life insurance to families. I have given sales presentations in the rarified air of boardrooms and in places so filthy that I wiped my feet on leaving, rather than on entering. I have been physically assaulted and thrown off a service station driveway for something which was not my fault; I have been kissed through the grateful tears of a widow when I brought her an unexpected and life-saving cheque.

We have seen it all, haven't we? We have sat through the product knowledge seminars, been exposed to the selling skills courses, seen the videos, done the role-playing, passed the tests and received the diplomas.

We know our products, our opposition, our customers. We are good at prospecting for new business. We may detest it but we know the value of up-to-date paperwork, and we knuckle down and keep the records, submit the reports and fill in the forms.

We do the job we are paid to do; almost always competently and at times with a sort of divinely inspired fury, but we do it.

We forget, sometimes, just how far we have come in selling, and it is only when we see and hear novice salespeople at work that we realise they are at the start of a road which we travelled a long time ago.

The biggest difference between the newcomer and us advanced salespeople is exactly the same difference as between the neophyte and the expert in sport. The novice golfer stands up to the ball with his mind a mish-mash of: 'Now, tuck the right elbow in, take the club slowly back for the first eighteen inches, slowly, *slowly* damn it, now keep your head back and slide your hips towards the target . . .' The expert stands up to the ball and says to himself: 'I am going to put my drive two hundred and thirty yards up the fairway and just to the left of the bunker.'

The new salesman starts his presentation with his mind full of things like: 'Now, make a good first impression on this customer; use the number three smile. Perhaps I should open with a Probing Question to get him involved and then go into

Intermediate Benefits, and let's not forget the Independent Third Person technique; that should work well here . . .'
The advanced salesperson starts his sales talk with only one thing in mind: 'This company has a real need for a specific product, and in the next twenty minutes I'm going to convince them that I have that product.'

The difference? In sport or selling, the newcomer is *technique*-oriented; the expert is *result*-oriented.

Think about it. That last successful sale you made, possibly against some pretty stiff opposition. Did you really go in with a list of techniques in your head and trot them out one by one? No, you did not. You said to yourself: 'The opposition will stress the fact that their replacement needles are much easier to install than ours. The customer will probably bring up the old objection about the anti-rust warranty. Okay, I'm ready for them.' Results, not techniques.

But does this mean that all that basic training we sat through was a waste of time? Doesn't the advanced salesperson use the techniques of selling?

The answer is yes, of course he does. He uses the basics of his craft just as the expert in every field of endeavour uses them. When Graham Gooch hits a drive through the covers he uses his feet to put himself in the proper position to deliver a solid blow to the ball. He was taught how to do this many years ago, but he doesn't have to *think* about his feet; he simply thinks about hitting the ball far enough away from the waiting hands of cover-point so that it speeds on its way to the boundary. He uses the techniques automatically.

You as an advanced salesperson do the same thing. You do the things you were taught – or that you taught yourself – long ago. You don't need to think about them, unless it happens that you find yourself not doing as well as you should. If your strike-rate in selling drops then it may well be that you need to go back to the basics, and the good salesperson is never too conceited to do just that.

But that is a temporary situation, and in the main you have no need to think about the basics because by now they have become second nature to you. Certainly, you don't need another book on sales techniques, and I wouldn't bother you with one. Why this, then?

[3]

A doctor who worked in a very busy hospital once told me that if the professors who had taught him in medical school could see the things which he and his overworked colleagues did, they would faint dead away with horror. I said, 'You're telling me that all those years of learning the medicine business were a waste of time?'

He said, 'No, of course not. You have to have the basics or you wouldn't know where to start. But once you have the solid knowledge of the ground rules you go on from there and find out when and how you can *break* those rules.'

I thought about this for a long time. At last it dawned on me that this is what the expert does. No matter what he does for a living he starts off as a new boy by having the rules of the game crammed down his throat. His teachers, mentors, guides or coaches instil in him a reverence for and an awe of the eternal verities, those Commandments of his business, sport or profession which have been carved in marble over the years by the wise, the learned, the savants. Those rules are sacrosanct, he is informed. Read, mark, learn and inwardly digest them, and ignore, forget or transgress them at your dire peril.

All well and good. When we enter into any discipline which is new and strange to us we need to be initiated into its mysteries. Sometimes the teaching period is a few days only; sometimes it can take years of full-time application and study. Whichever, our noses are kept to the grindstone and if we ever do a thing which is not exactly as we were taught we hear all about it.

You can surely remember back in the days when you were an out-of-the-box new salesman, making a sales call with your manager or trainer at your side, watching and listening to your every word and move. Do you remember how after the call you were told something like: 'Not bad, lad (or lass), but there was one part where you didn't do it according to the book. We'll have to practise that until you can do it in your sleep.'

Techniques, techniques; always techniques, and always exactly according to the rules. Trap the ball with the inside of the foot. Never have a 'busy' advertisement; keep it simple. Never draw blood from an artery; always a vein. Don't call on a customer in his lunch-hour. Pink and orange clash, so never wear them together. Attack the enemy by diving out of the

[4]

sun. Everyone hates a dictatorial manager – be permissive and participative with your staff. Always buy into a rising market, never a falling one. Stay clear of junk food – it's poison. Don't ever interrupt the prospect.

All drilled into the newcomer and all, no doubt, solid and reliable pearls of wisdom. It will probably take the newcomer years to realise that these rules can be broken – indeed, *must* be broken if in this special situation, dealing with this special person or problem, we are to achieve our goal.

This book is about breaking the rules in selling, and it is intended only for you, the advanced salesperson. If I could I'd make it illegal for any new salespeople to read it, because if they did they might be tempted to try their hands at some of the suggestions, and they might just come the most fearful cropper.

Incidentally, I used the word 'suggestions' there, and that is all this book consists of. You are an experienced, senior salesperson, bearing the honourable scars of many encounters in the selling arena, and you would not be very impressed if I tried to lay down the law to you, so I don't. I say in these pages: 'What do you think of this? What if you tried it that way? Have you ever thought of doing it like that?' That's all; you accept or reject the suggestions as you please. You may find here a new angle on something in selling which has bothered you from time to time, or at the very least you will be able to sit back and see what other advanced salespeople did when they found that in order to make the sale they had to break the rules.

Chapter 1

KINDERGARTEN: WHEN WE WERE VERY YOUNG

Let's go back to that first sales course we ever attended. Remember it? The conference room with the projectors and whiteboards and flipcharts and flannelboards, the sales trainer with his polished delivery and clever jokes, the role-playing – quite nerve-racking in the beginning but turned out to be very good fun, the question time when you tried to think up intelligent questions to ask, the interesting and ingenious techniques which were intended to get the prospective customer to agree to this, to concede to that, to sign the order.

Then the diploma which told the world that 'This is to certify that Charlie GREENHORN has attended the STAR SELLING SEMINAR and has attained the standards required to be called a STAR SALESMAN'. It was a nice thing to have, although you noticed that every delegate got one, so there were no failures, which was reasonable, since there had been no examination to pass or fail. Anyway, you put the diploma in a drawer and promised yourself that as soon as you had an office of your own you would have it framed and hang it up on the wall. (You never did; by the time you had your own office you laughed at the idea of displaying a piece of paper saying that you had attended a sales course.)

That was how it was, wasn't it? The sales trainer was so very *positive* about everything. 'Don't worry about the price objection; the customer will always pay the price so long as you sell him the quality.' He calmed your fears, told you that salesmen are not born, they are made. 'There is no one in this room who can't be a millionaire in the selling profession!' He shook each delegate's hand and wished him all the luck in the world. 'Just remember, if you can think it, you can do it!'

Great stuff.

Armed with all that knowledge and expertise you went out into the real world. You made your first solo flight into selling without the protection of your sales manager; you called on your first customer. Accoutred with a briefcase, virgin order book, catalogues, samples, demonstration kit, customer complaint forms and a breath-sweetening spray, you bore more than a passing resemblance to an army pack-mule.

You found that it was nothing like you expected. First, with very few exceptions, people were not actively rude. They could be busy, uninterested or curt, but they didn't lay hands on you and throw you out. They didn't shout personal insults at you. However, the actual sales call was very different from those fascinating customer/salesman games in the sales training session. The main difference was that the prospect didn't really participate. You didn't get long, well-constructed sentences from him as you saw on the training videos. He didn't say: 'That's very interesting, Mr Smith [that's you]; so you tell me that if I buy your tangential orthicons, they will lower my blood pressure, put my son through university and take the weeds out of my lawn? I'll certainly take a gross of them, and thank you very much for calling!'

He didn't talk like that in real life. He didn't make sentences. He grunted:

'We tried that. Doesn't work.'

'Not this month, thanks.'

'Doesn't look too bad.'

'Yes, it seems to do the job all right.'

'Not this week, thanks.'

'Okay, but only half a dozen.'

'Same as last time, please.'

So the first problem you encountered was to get any coherent reaction from the prospect.

You found other things very different from what you were taught. Some techniques did work very well, if used on the right person at the right time. Others sounded terribly artificial, and people looked at you as though you had grown a third ear. You quickly stopped using anything which didn't fit into your selling 'personality' as it were, and you found that you were indeed developing such a personality, exclusive to you. You found that one salesperson could use a technique which another could not; you could say something which worked very well while I might find that it merely embarrassed me and alienated the listener.

So you went, discarding some things and incorporating others until you had your own armoury of methods and techniques which worked for you. You realised that you had come a long way from that first training course and looking back you saw how unrealistic many of the things were which were given to you as being pillars of the selling process. Nevertheless, you were grateful that you had been able to attend the course because in the early days as a cub salesperson it did at least give you a track to run on. But just as my doctor friend found that once he was in the real world of medicine as distinct from the cloistered halls of medical school he had to forget a lot of what had been drummed into him if he was to do a competent job, so you as an advanced salesperson found that a lot of what you had been taught had to be forgotten – or at least changed radically – if you were to be really successful in selling.

Now, none of this is meant as a smear on sales training. I'm a sales trainer and I believe in what I do. I work with all sorts and levels of salespeople – some so new and raw that we have to break for their four-hourly feeds, some so old in sin that they wouldn't believe me if I told them the time by their own watches. Sales training works, and it is useful at all stages of experience and expertise. It lays down rules which give the novice a jumping-off place, somewhere to start. Without it he or she would be completely at sea, with nothing to cling to. Because of this they would also be terrified – it's not too strong a word – so basic training also instils *confidence*, without which they probably wouldn't have the courage to knock on that first door.

No, the basics are essential, the rules must be learnt. It is only much later, when we have found our feet in selling, that these rules can be broken and in some cases must be broken, if we are to move from mere adequacy in selling to star performance.

I have taken longer than I usually do over the preamble in this book, but that is because we are engaged in an unusual job here. Most manuals in any discipline set out the rules to follow; this one will set up rules only to knock them down. It was necessary to explain why.

All right, let's see how many of the sacred cows of the selling business we can destroy.

Chapter 2

BE A NOSEY PARKER

Be discreet, we were told. Don't give the customer the feeling that you are sticking your nose into his business. Don't ask intrusive questions, you'll only annoy him. Have the good taste to respect his privacy. Don't pry. You will close the door to future sales if you act like a snoop.

Good rule, no doubt about it. Interesting, too, because it is a rule of *behaviour*. It is saying, show the customer that you know how to act, that you have good business manners.

Well, how can you break a rule like that? Not only will you antagonise the customer, you won't even have the right to call yourself a professional salesperson.

Perhaps so, but let's see what a very fine salesman – and a great gentleman – once had to say about it. Six months after I had joined the Parker Pen Company the great Kenneth Parker himself came over to my country. By a weird sequence of events – my manager had broken his ankle, and *his* manager had had to go to Australia where his mother was very ill – it fell to me to meet the boss man of the Parker Pen Company off his luxury liner and take him to his hotel.

As we drove through town, I saw that Mr Parker was looking this way and that, and I began pointing out some of the interesting places in the town where I was born. Kenneth Parker wasn't interested in the interesting places. He was looking at shop windows. It happened that a minor traffic jam had brought us to a halt right opposite a large stationery store, and his eyes fastened on the window displays. He said, 'Does that store stock our pens, Michael?'

I was flattered at being included in the ownership of the

Parker Pen Company; 'our pens' was a nice way of putting it.
I said, 'Oh, yes, indeed, sir. They certainly do.'

He said, 'Which models?'

'The fifty-one, the Major and the Junior.'

He nodded. 'What other pens do they stock?'

I hesitated. 'Schaeffer, and I think Watermans and Conway
Stewart.'

'Inks?'

I was beginning to wish that the cars in front would move so
that this line of questioning would stop. 'Er – well, ours, of
course. I think I've seen some Scrip there, too.'

'Who is the buyer for pens?'

At least I knew the answer to that one. 'Mr Henderson.'

'What's his first name?'

'His – ' I said, 'I'm not on first-name terms with him. I
think we are more formal with customers than you are on your
side of the Atlantic, sir.'

Mr Parker said, 'I guess so.' He was still looking at the
window. 'I see they sell typewriters. What make?'

A desperate look at the window showed me a small name on
a display board. 'Underwood.'

'Would they have exclusivity?'

'*Exclusivity*, Mr Parker?'

He said patiently. 'Yes. Would they be part of a chain of
stores which has the Underwood franchise?'

After six months in business I didn't really know what a
franchise was, except that it sounded like a good thing to have.
I was tempted to bluff my way through this problem but the
little I had seen of Mr Parker gave me the idea that he was not
the sort of person who would be easily bluffed. I said, 'I don't
know.'

'Do they do their own servicing of typewriters, or do they
send them to the Underwood agents?'

Why is there never a traffic policeman when you really want
one? I gave up. I said, 'Mr Parker, these are typewriter
questions. I'm sorry to sound so ignorant, but I'm in the
fountain-pen business, remember?'

Kenneth Parker said gently, 'Michael, until you know the
answers to questions like that, you aren't in the fountain-pen
business. That store is your life-blood in business; that one

and hundreds like it. Without them you die. Now, in order to do a half-way decent job of selling to them you have to know every single thing you can about them.'

The traffic jam slowly dissolved and we were on our way again. I said, 'Yes, I can see that. But you asked me what the buyer's first name was and I didn't know. Do I need to know? As it happens, he is a reserved, stiff sort of character, and there isn't a chance in a thousand that I'll ever be on first-name terms with him.'

'Don't be so sure of that, but even so, you should know it. There are two sorts of information you should have about your customer – personal and company. Company comes first, of course, and you may be surprised at what you should know about *his* business which you may consider is none of *your* business.'

It was easy talking to this great man, especially now that the catechism was over. 'Such as what?'

He said, 'Well, I was talking to a man on the way over here whose company sells heavy trucks. He said that one of the questions his salesmen ask a fleet operator is: "How many of your drivers quit their jobs every year?" '

I said, 'That's an intrusive question. If I was the operator I would tell him it was none of his business.'

Mr Parker nodded in agreement. 'That's the reaction his salesmen often do get.'

'Then what?'

'Then the salesman has to point out that if he is not about to waste the customer's time he has to *make* it his business. Well, you don't win them all, but most of them are curious enough to say something like, "I lose about twenty per cent of my men every year; so what?" '

I had also felt like saying, 'So what?' but I kept my mouth shut.

'So the salesman says, "That's too much; that's costing you a fortune," and he proves to the customer that hiring, training and supervising one driver in five every year is indeed costing him big bucks.' Kenneth Parker looked at me. I thought that there had to be something I could say which would show that I was following this story intelligently. I said nothing. He went on: 'So the salesman shows the trucker the results of a survey which proves that most drivers believe that his truck is safer than any other. He demonstrates that there are more adjustments to the driving seat of the truck than there are to the seats of most luxury cars; that noise levels, vibration, visibility are better than other trucks – ' Mr Parker opened his hand. 'Well, you get the idea. He is right into a very powerful, hard-hitting sales presentation.'

I said, 'Yes, I see that.'

'But do you also see that it would have been impossible to give that presentation unless he had stuck his nose into the customer's business?' He paused. 'You told me that what the salesman asked the trucker was an intrusive question; it was. Michael, when you go to see Mr Henderson in that stationery store, that isn't a social call. He is a busy man, and the only justification for taking up his time is the possibility that you are going to increase his profits, cut his losses, or somehow make his life easier. How can you hope to do any of those things if you don't ask intrusive questions?'

I'm not stupid; if you explain it slowly, using short words, I get the message eventually. I said, 'All right, I accept that. But that sort of intimate knowledge of a customer's affairs is on the business side. You aren't going to tell me that I have to stick my nose into his private life, surely.'

Mr Parker raised his eyebrows. 'Well, you don't walk into his office with a clipboard and say, "I'm doing a customer survey, sir. How many children do you have and what are your drinking habits?" '

I heaved a sigh of relief. It turned out to be premature. 'However, Michael, you do need to know everything you can about Mr Henderson, and I mean everything. You may not ask him straight out, and of course you don't get it all at once, but if you *could* find out that he is a lay preacher, that he has a pregnant bull terrier, that he is allergic to pollen, that he loves big-band swing and collects snuff-boxes, well, that puts you on the inside track with him.'

I felt a strong sense of disappointment. So the boss of one of the largest companies of its kind in the world actually believed that tired old rubbish that you should find out what the customer's hobby is and then get him talking about it and thus get into his good books. I said, 'You mean if I find that he

[13]

breeds racing pigeons or builds model aircraft I should go to the library and read up about it and get closer to him that way.' Even new as I was, with hardly any selling experience, I didn't believe it.

He said, 'No, no, no. Do that and you will land on your nose. He will quickly see that you have no real depth knowledge of the subject, and therefore no real interest in it. No, I mean the more you know about a person the more you understand that person. When you know something of that person's background, his interests, his likes and dislikes, then he becomes three-dimensional. Then he isn't just Mr Henderson, pen buyer of the Southern Stationery Stores; he becomes Andy Henderson, just about to become a director of the Southern chain, keen amateur photographer, an innovator with exciting ideas about modernising the Southern stores, and married to the chairperson of the local Heart Foundation.'

I understood. 'He's flesh and blood, not just a cardboard cut-out. I can communicate with him.'

'Right!'

Mr Parker was generous with his time and I spent many hours with him, taking him around, introducing him to people. I blessed my manager's broken ankle while I learnt from this man. I came back to the subject of customer knowledge while I was driving him to see some potential office accommodation. I said, 'You said that there were two aspects to sticking your nose into a customer's affairs: personal and business. All right, you explained the personal side. Now, I can see that it would help me to know everything there is to know about his business, but the idea of asking him about things which most people consider confidential simply scares me. That was a good example about the truck salesmen, but I'm really worried about putting the customer's back up.'

He said, 'Yes, that's understandable, and sometimes it isn't easy.'

I said, 'Take yourself, sir. I am a raw novice at selling and I'm not even twenty-one years old. How far would I get if I walked into your office and started asking questions about the way you run your company?'

Kenneth Parker smiled. 'Not very far at first, certainly. But when you had called a few times, when you had proved to me

[14]

that you were no blabbermouth, that you could be trusted with confidential information and, most importantly, that you had to have that information in order to do a better selling job to my company – then you would get quite far.'

A few years ago I was invited to run a series of training clinics for the middle managers of a large industrial company. A few weeks before that the company had been exposed to the sort of publicity any manager dreads; one of its senior people had shot himself in his office just before serious charges were to be brought against him.

I was discussing the forthcoming training with three top managers in the head office building and I knew that there was a question I simply had to ask. I didn't want to ask it, Lord knows. I said, 'Please tell me about the death of your director.'

Well, the temperature in that room went down about twenty degrees. I knew that I was inches from the training series being cancelled and being told that I could leave. Someone said, 'That has nothing to do with the subject we are discussing.'

I said, 'Gentlemen, I'm sorry, but I have to know about it. Not the details of the tragedy itself, but how it has affected staff morale and particularly, what difference it has made to the situation of the managers I am going to be working with.'

I remember that one of the directors resisted the thought that the incident could possibly have anything to do with my work; it was obviously a very sore point with him. They asked me to leave the room while they discussed it and when I came back in I could see that one man was still very unhappy about it. Anyway, they told me all about it and how their people felt. One of them conceded that the shock effect was still very apparent in many of the staff and that there had even been two resignations, obviously linked to the sad affair.

I said, 'You can imagine that I did not want to bring this business up, but I shall be getting very close to your middle managers and they are almost certain to mention it in discussion periods. When they do I simply have to know about it.' I pointed out the fact that as an outsider I might be able to discuss it objectively and dispassionately, and perhaps pour some oil on the troubled waters of staff indecision and low company esteem.

In fact, that was exactly what happened, and after the series the marketing director called me and acknowledged that the clinics seemed to have had a side-effect of putting the whole thing in perspective for their managers. He said, 'You know, Mr Beer, you shocked us when you first brought it up.'

I said, 'You nearly threw me out, didn't you?'

He said, 'Very nearly. You seemed to be sticking your nose into something which didn't concern you – and which flicked us on the raw. Anyway, as it happened, it turned out for the best.'

I thanked him for his confidence in me. He said, 'Not at all. In fact one reason I called you was to say that we have decided, since you know all the skeletons in our company cupboard, to get you to run another series, this one for our internal people – it seems that you are the obvious choice.'

And that, very often, is what happens. Get to know everything about the customer, get deep inside it, pry, snoop, be a Nosey Parker and a Peeping Tom – and the customer begins to realise that since you are practically a part of the company it makes sense to do business with you. It is incredible how the attitude towards you can change. You find them accepting much more readily what you recommend in the way of products and services. The final indication that you have broken through is that they call you and ask your advice before taking action on something which affects one of your products.

'Kevin, we are thinking of switching to three-drum sanders. You know the sort of problems we have been having with the two-drum machines. Now, before we make a final decision, if we change over, can we still use your garnet open-coat paper on the three-drum machines? If we can't I'm not changing.'

'Mr Fairlie, when you were here last week you asked me why we gave so much space to our house brand of fruit juice. I may have sounded a bit off-hand, because I thought you were trying to teach me my job, but since then I have been thinking that I may be doing something wrong. Could you come in again and discuss it?'

'Louise, you are always so darned inquisitive about our business; come and have a look at the new layout in our computer room and tell us what you think.'

The trick here, and it is truly the whole trick, is to show them that you are sticking your nose into their business because only in that way can you really help them. You should be able to show how you were able to help other people in similar situations. You must convince them of your integrity and complete discretion – that nothing you learn about them or their companies, their production methods, their marketing strategies will ever, ever, be revealed to a living soul. This is vital because your customer is not stupid and he knows that you also call on his opposition. It isn't easy to break down the natural barriers of reticence and reserve, but when you show why it is necessary, and when they see positive proof that you have been able to help them precisely because of your in-depth knowledge of how they operate, it becomes easier and easier until they actually begin to volunteer information without being asked.

The results? First, you find that you have the inside track on *all* other suppliers. They are standing with their noses pressed against the sweet-shop window while you are inside enjoying the goodies. Second, and this is more important than it may sound, you gain stature in the eyes of the customer. He sees you as someone who is interested in more than merely walking in with a sample and walking out with an order. He realises that he is dealing with a professional, one who makes it his business to know his customer's business and who can therefore sell to the customer's specific needs.

Break the rule – stick your nose into his business.

Chapter 3

_____

THINK *SMALL*

Think big, we are urged. Look at the big picture and make your customer do the same thing. After all, if the salesperson thinks small, so will the customer, and sales will be small, too. Don't get bogged down in detail in your sales presentation; paint with a broad brush. Your customer will respect and admire you if you can show him how dramatically and excitingly different your product is from all other products. A salesperson is as big as he thinks – and his sales volume follows the same rule.

I would be the last person to try and talk anyone out of thinking big. As a one-time sales manager I found that a lot of the problems I had with my people was because I couldn't get them to see the big picture. Yet there are times when we have to break this excellent rule, when by thinking big we can lose the sale and by thinking small we can win it.

First we need to look at what has happened over the years to the products we sell. One would think, with all the research and development, the high technology available these days, that products would be very different, one from the other, that there would be significant and easily demonstrable differences between your product and the one across the road. Yet when we examine the products closely and if we are completely honest we find that there is often a depressing similarity between them; oddly enough, it is that same technology which has produced this sameness.

Take cars. When I was a little tadpole of twelve, I could hang over our gate and say, 'Daddy, there's a Morris; that's an Austin, Daddy; there's a Rover.' Not so easy for today's small boy, is it? All cars are designed in wind tunnels and on computer screens, and their shapes are difficult to tell apart. In the smaller car category at least, they are all heading towards front-wheel drive, single overhead camshafts, double braking systems and independent all-round suspension. They are good products, too; a car doesn't stay in the market-place for long these days if it isn't well designed and constructed.

So when the hype and euphoria of the launch party is over the car salesman looks at his new product and asks himself, 'Hell, how do I sell this against those other guys when there really isn't anything exciting or dramatic that I can show customers?'

Wouldn't it be nice if we could always show customers that our product had a real, solid, big advantage – something that made it ten per cent better than the opposition? Often these days that ten per cent is hard to find, but let me show you something interesting:

You don't have a ten per cent advantage? Then find ten *one* per cent advantages, because they come to the same thing. In the customer's mind they weigh the same as the big exciting thing which we recognise is just not possible to find.

Break the rule, think small, and win the sale.

The thing is that if there does happen to be a ten per cent advantage it certainly doesn't take the expertise of an advanced salesperson to find it; it is usually so obvious that any new salesperson can spot it. The little one per cents, now; that's a very different thing. Often they are so small and apparently unimportant that it takes an advanced salesperson to *find* them, let alone show their worth in a sales presentation.

Another thing: when you have a price *disadvantage*, when your product costs more than the opposition and to the customer they seem to be much the same in design and performance, only thinking small can possibly help.

[19]

This is what it looks like to the customer. You have a ten per cent price disadvantage:

There is no ten per cent for us to stick on our side of the scale, so we think small:

'Ms Preston, you tell me that you send a lot of manuscripts over to America. This model copier can reduce the print size from A4 to A5 – that's a real saving of many pounds in postage.'

(Call that three per cent in the customer's mind):

'I see that you have a duplicating machine in the corner there. When you have this XP-90 installed you can get rid of it because the new machine will do everything the duplicator can do, and faster and cleaner, too.'

(Let's say that's worth another two per cent):

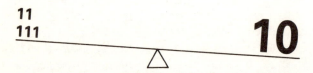

'Did I say that the XP-90 can also make overhead projector transparencies? Very useful bonus, that, and your advertising and training departments will love it.'

(That's surely worth another two per cent):

'A big word these days is standardisation. Our extensive dealer network means that no matter where you are we have a depot where we can service your machines. You can transfer a machine to another office with no worries.'

(For the right customer that could easily be worth three per cent):

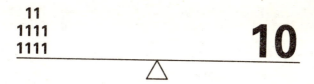

'You can order your paper supplies in bulk to get the best discount and we'll keep what you don't need until you tell us to deliver – this saves you storage space and money.'

(At least one per cent – and it's all we need):

Break the rule – think *small*, sell *big*.

Chapter 4

TALK TO THE *WRONG* PEOPLE

I once read a statement in a journal on salesmanship which said: 'Industrial salesmen spend two-thirds of their time talking to the wrong people.'

Wow. That's a sweeping announcement, and if it is true then industrial salesmen are in deep trouble. Think of it – forty minutes out of every selling hour the salesperson is wasting his time. And note, that is out of every *selling* hour, and we all know (because it has been hammered into us) that out of a normal selling day the average salesperson spends not more than a couple of hours at the most in eyeball-to-eyeball selling. So if we as industrial salespeople are wasting two-thirds of those precious couple of hours we are not only in trouble, we all ought to be in jail for taking money from our companies.

What is the rule? What did they teach us under the heading *Self-organisation*, sub-heading: *Time and territory planning*? They said, search diligently for the one person who can say 'Yes' to your sales presentation. Don't be put off by assistants or deputies or secretaries or foremen or receptionists or juniors or nightwatchmen; find the one person who has the authority to sign your order and sell the hell out of him!

That's the rule, and it's a good one, no question about it. You can't sell unless you are talking to the person or panel or committee or board or decision-maker of some sort or other. It's a good rule.

Let's break it.

First, let's go back to the opening statement about industrial sales*people*. (Lots of women sell industrial products.)

[22]

Why single out industrial salespeople? Let's lump all salespeople into this indictment, because indictment is what it is, of course. Surely any person selling anything can find himself talking to the wrong person, can't he?

Brief pause here while you think of someone selling to someone, and he knows without any doubt whatever that he is selling to the right person, so that you can throw it in my face. I'll give you an example which really happened. Suppose you sell carpeting and you are talking to Charlie Bachelor in his one-roomed flat about carpeting the one room. Charlie lives alone, has no steady girl-friend to influence his decision, and he has no uncle in the carpeting business. You are talking to the right person, right? Must be – there is no one else. You give your sales talk your best shot, but Charlie puts you off and you find out later that he has bought from another supplier.

Why? Because you were talking to the wrong person. As it happens, Charlie's mother runs Charlie's life to the extent that he consults her as to when he should change over to winter underwear. You should have been talking to Mama Bachelor, you yo-yo. Believe it, any salesperson can talk to the wrong person without knowing it, so the rule about sparing no effort to find the right person is indeed a good one.

We are going to break the rule, but the difference between us and the luckless carpet salesman is that he didn't know he was talking to the wrong person; we are going to do it deliberately.

We are going to find the people who can't buy, the ones without the authority to sign the order. We shall search these people out, find them at any cost, get as much information on them as we can, and *talk* to them.

Why? Well, here's what happened to one of my salesmen when he talked to the *right* person. He was in the coated abrasive division of the company. One day he turned up at the office of an engineer of an automotive assembly plant. The libretto went something like this:

'Mr Abney, our people have developed a marvellous new sanding disc.'

'What's so marvellous about it, and what does it cost?'

'It costs about ten per cent more than you are paying now,

but – '

'Oh, that's marvellous, all right. That's really marvellous.' Engineers can be heavily sarcastic.

'No, sir; what's marvellous is that it lasts twenty per cent longer than the discs you are using now.'

Well, it hardly needs a mathematical genius to calculate that something which costs ten per cent more and lasts twenty per cent longer is very good value. My salesman was all ready to demonstrate his product in a comparison test, but this engineer was one of those sceptical types – another characteristic of the breed – who believed something only when it was shown to work on the job itself. He had had good products and service from our company in the past, so he said, 'All right, we'll try it for one month on that small assembly line in the corner. Send me three cases of it. Goodbye.' Conversation over.

At the end of the month my man broke all speed records back to the plant, expecting a big order for the new disc which he knew was a winner. He said, 'How did it go, Mr Abney? Pretty good product, isn't it? I was right about it, wasn't I?'

The engineer said, 'Well, I'll tell you. You were exactly *half* right. I got your account for the three cases you sent me and no question about it, it does cost ten per cent more than the discs I use now. Trouble is, it doesn't last any longer than the old discs, and they cost ten per cent less. Goodbye.' Conversation over.

The salesman was shocked and bewildered. He knew that the discs lasted longer; extensive tests had proved this. What had gone wrong?

Well, what had gone wrong was that he had obeyed the rule which said, find the right person, the one who can say 'Yes' to your sales presentation, and sell to him. His mistake was in not looking for the wrong person, the one who had no authority to buy, and talking to him. In this case the wrong person did not sit in an office at the end of the factory; no, he wore overalls and safety goggles and used a pneumatic grinder. Nobody talked to him, you see. Nobody bothered to say to him, 'Hey, Curly; you know that you have been using five discs along the side panels of a car body? Well, now you only have to use four of the discs – these new ones last longer.'

[24]

So, Curly stopped the grinder at the usual place along the panel, snapped off the old disc as he had been doing for years, and clicked on a new one. He knew that it took five discs; it always had.

My salesman did eventually get the business at that factory, but only after he had sought out the wrong person, the person who couldn't buy, and talked to him.

These people are all over the place, of course. A salesman for pesticides managed to get on the wrong side of a sub-manager on a fruit farm. It was a little thing – he had called to see the manager who was away at the time, and when the sub-manager asked politely if he could help, the salesman was just a shade condescending. He dealt only at senior level, you see.

Well, it wasn't long afterwards that the sales records showed that the farm had stopped buying one of the company's most effective pesticides, a wettable powder for the control of codling moth. The salesman knew that the farm had had good results with this product in the past and he rushed around to see the general manager and stick his finger in the dyke. It was too late; the farm had switched over to an opposition powder which killed the nasties just as well as the old powder.

'But why did you change?' the salesman asked. 'You were quite happy with our product.'

'Yes, we were,' the general manager said. 'But then you changed the formula, and the new product isn't as good.'

'B-but we *haven't* changed it,' the salesman protested. 'It's the same as it always was.'

'You must have changed it somehow,' was the curt reply. 'My sub-manager informs me that the product is now clogging the nozzles. The powder doesn't seem to go into suspension properly, and my sub-manager says that they are spending hours cleaning the lines. He is having no trouble at all with the powder from your opposition.'

Of *course* the sub-manager is having no trouble with the opposition product – probably because the opposition salesman talked to him, the man who couldn't buy. The company never did get that one back.

So far we have had examples of industrial and agricultural salespeople, both of them end-user selling situations. What

[25]

about the re-seller business, the people who sell to shops, chainstores, pharmacists and supermarkets; can we go wrong by talking to the right people? We can indeed.

The shelf-packer in a supermarket is the wrong person to talk to. He has no power to sign an order, he can't even recommend one product over another to his manager. He is, regrettably, the least important person in the place. Why talk to him?

We talk to him because to us he is the most important wrong person in the whole building. His manager buys our toothpaste and pickles and baby foods and shampoos, and all the packer has to do is put them on the shelves. But how carefully does he pack them? Does he bother about rotating the stock, so that our jelly beans are always fresh? Is he always alert to replenish our stocks from the store-room, so that our display exerts the most shelf pressure on the customer? Does he remove damaged stock and keep it for us when we call?

Why should he do any of this for us? After all, he is not a very highly paid worker and, we can assume, not a very highly motivated person. Why should he cast a watchful and friendly eye on our products as he passes the shelves? Because some time ago we had the brilliant if unconventional idea of treating him like a human being. The occasional jar after work, a box of choccies for his wife, a word of appreciation for putting our tumble-pack in a favourable place – that's all it takes.

But why bother, says the novice salesman. I've been told not to waste time on my calls. I see the person who can say 'Yes'.

One more example of talking to the wrong person. I was working with a group of salespeople in the OTC drugs business. OTC, as if you didn't know (you are an advanced salesperson, or you shouldn't be reading this), is Over The Counter, meaning that you don't need a prescription to buy them. The product was multi-vitamin pills. It was a good product, with all the necessary vitamins – A, B-complex, C, D, E, all the way to Z or whatever. The problem was that there were at least seven other pills on the market, all with the A to Z vitamins, and all at the same price.

So the salespeople talked to the right person, in this case, the pharmacist himself. The pharmacist looked at the product with a jaundiced eye – he already had seven brands of vitamin pills on his shelves – saw that the formulation was about the same as all the others, and turned up his nose. The salespeople were ready for this reaction, however. They explained that with the saturation TV advertising, the coupon offers, the competition with a car as the first prize, people were going to be asking for the pills and would expect them to be in his pharmacy.

So, albeit without his pulse-rate quickening with excitement, the pharmacist bought a couple of cases. He was the right person, of course; he had the authority to buy and he was the only one who did. The cases were duly delivered and the bottles of pills were unpacked and put on the shelves. Where, after some initial interest by the public because of the special offers and the contest, they sat. Oh, they sold, after a fashion, but there was plenty of choice of vitamin pills and they didn't exactly walk out of the shop.

What to do? The salespeople had talked to the right person, but perhaps he was only the right person when it came to buying the pills. The trouble was that he *bought* them, he didn't *sell* them. He was usually busy in his dispensary or with some administrative details. Only in the rush-hour did he actually come and serve behind the counters, and then he usually had to ask his assistants where on *earth* do we keep the broncho-dilators these days?

Ah – his assistants. The wrong people, surely; no authority to buy. Can they help us by *selling* if they can't help by buying? Well, let us stand discreetly to one side and watch these assistants at work. What do we see? Let us concentrate on antacid tablets, for instance. Plenty of different makes, lots of competition. Now, when a customer asks specifically for a certain brand of tablet she gets it without question; there is no attempt on the part of the assistant to change the customer over to another brand. Why should there be, after all? There is no incentive to do so, and the shop is busy, with no time for a long sales talk.

But suppose someone comes in and says, 'My heartburn is killing me; please give me something to fix it.' Now it is entirely up to the assistant as to which brand she sells to the customer. What does she do? She reaches for a packet or bottle of tablets and, do you see, they are the ones which are *nearest* to her. Why not? Why should she trek a whole three paces to where another brand is displayed? 'These are fine,' she says, and the sale is made.

So the first thing we see is that, as usual in retail selling, the great and powerful god Location dictates how a product moves out of a store. This is interesting and valuable information, but as advanced salespeople we already know all about location of product. Also, it doesn't help us to move our vitamin pills, because we see that in the case of this pharmacy all the vitamin products are neatly grouped behind the cash register, so all the assistant has to do is reach behind her and all the different brands are ready to hand.

Will it help if we talk to her? Let us recognise that she has no motivation to sell one product over another. If we are honest we must acknowledge, if only to ourselves, that there is little difference between our product and the opposition – they all do about the same job. If we are realistic we know that there is no way to turn the Suzy or Harry behind that counter into a hotshot, enthusiastic salesperson of our pill. They are completely the wrong people to talk to, so let's break the rule and talk to them.

What can we say to persuade them to reach for our brand when someone comes in and says, 'I'm really not feeling up to scratch and I think I need some vitamins; which are the best?'

Well, first, as in the case of the shelf-packer in the previous example, we can treat them with friendliness and respect. We don't simply walk past them and talk only with the pharmacist, we stop and talk to them as equals. Standing behind a counter, slowly getting dropped metatarsal arches and low back pain is not the most prestigious job in the world, and a friendly word or an interested question can make the day a touch less dreary. Such a simple point, but how often do we forget it?

However, there is something much more important we can talk about and here we use a characteristic which every single human being possesses: *we all like to be the expert*. We love knowing something which other people don't know, and we like to talk about that something. You are a photography buff? If I ask you, 'Please tell me, what is the advantage of a

[28]

single-lens reflex camera over a twin-lens?' you will back me into a corner and you won't let me go until you have told me more than I want to know about cameras.

So, without trying to turn Suzy or Harry into experts on our product, can we give them one tiny piece of information which they don't have about the other products? We pondered this problem in the conference, the group and I. We hadn't really got anywhere when I opened a bottle of the pills and threw some out onto the table. They looked about the same as any other pill; nothing exciting there. We bounced some thoughts around without getting anywhere and I absently popped one of the pills into my mouth. I said, 'It isn't sweet.'

By this time the group was becoming a trifle bored, and someone said disgustedly, 'You're not supposed to suck it, Michael; it isn't a sweet.'

One of the group sat up suddenly. 'Wait a minute, *wait* a minute,' she said. 'It isn't a sweet and it isn't sweet. There's no sugar-coating on it – and all the other pills are sugar-coated.'

There it was – the special something which we could tell the counter people, the wrong people. It wasn't a big or dramatic thing but it made them, in a small way, the experts. Now, when someone asked them, 'Which vitamin pills are the best?', they could say, 'You know, they are all good, but this one is especially made for anyone with a sugar problem, or if you are on a diet. There's no sugar in the coating.'

This sort of thing *works*. It works because most salespeople don't bother to talk to the assistants, the storemen, the packers, the artisans, the drivers, the sweepers or the lad who polishes the handle of the big front door.

We don't need to be reminded, do we, that it is necessary to ask the permission of the right person before we talk to the wrong people; we have to clear it with the boss before we can spend time with the assistants. This is simple good manners.

Break the rule and talk to the wrong people – and sell where there was no sale.

Chapter 5

SELL THEM WHAT THEY HAVE NO USE FOR

One of the first things to do when prospecting for new business, so the rule says, is to find out what they use which you can sell them. You have to qualify them, don't you? If you don't do this, you will never know if you have a prospect on your hands.

Suppose you sell fastenings. You do some research on your target and you find from an examination of the products he makes that he uses size 7 snap fasteners, half-inch non-ferrous staples, and a weird-looking cross between a screw and a nail which you have never seen before. Well, fine; you don't sell the odd-looking screw-nail, but you are certainly in the business of snap fasteners of all sizes and staples, ferrous and non-ferrous, so it certainly looks as though you have a prospect. The rule says, find out what he uses in his business, know your opposition so that you can point out the advantages which your products have over those he is using now, and go for it.

Well, that seems like a very sound rule, so let's break it.

A salesman once told me that when he joined the staff of a company which sold industrial plastic tape, he nearly resigned in despair after the first three weeks. It had been explained to him that his value to his new company would be in direct proportion to the amount of new business he brought in, and he simply wasn't getting any new business. He was working hard enough, Lord knew; driving to industrial townships, parking his car, tramping from factory to factory and talking to engineers, managers, foremen and technicians, searching for people who used the products which he represented.

He found two types of factory: the ones which didn't use tape at all, and the ones which did, but were already customers of his company for at least one or two of his products. (It does sound as though his company had a basic organisation problem if he did not know which companies were already customers before he called on them, but that is another story.)

He was sitting one evening, going through his call report of that day and wondering why he was such a dead loss as a prospector. Flicking through his prospect cards, he frowned; here was a company in the business of making components for audio equipment – tape decks, speakers, turntables. To his question, 'Do you use any plastic tape in your factory at all?', the answer had been, 'Sorry, no. We have no use for that sort of thing.'

All right, but a few days ago he had called on a company in exactly the same business. Where was their card? Here you are, and look at that, will you? They use *three* different types of tape. Not only that, but they buy all three tapes from us, and not only *that*, but the manager had told him that they would be lost without those products!

Feeling that he had something very important by the tail, the salesman went over the approach he had been using on his prospecting calls. He realised that he had been introducing himself and his company and had then gone on to say something like this: 'We make plastic tape for all sorts of applications in industry. Tell me, do you use any tape in your manufacturing process?'

That was where he was going wrong. He was following the rule which says *find out what he is using; if you sell that product then he is a prospect*. Fine, and what a good rule. The trouble with it is that if you turn it over and look at the flip-side, then it says if he *doesn't* use what you sell then he *isn't* a prospect.

Which is nonsense.

The salesman did two things. First, he vowed that he would never again start a sales call by asking, 'Do you use our sort of product?' Second, he searched through business directories to find other companies which made audio equipment; he found five. The next day he called on those five, and he was lucky with his first call because when he had introduced himself and his company the engineer said, 'Oh, yes, we use one of your products. Excellent stuff.'

The salesman sent up a short prayer of thanks to his guardian angel and said, 'Do you mind if I see how you use it? I'm new to the company and I'm not familiar with all the applications of our products.'

'With pleasure. Come along.' The tape was a sophisticated product made of polyurethane foam with an adhesive on both sides. The salesman was shown how the factory used it to fasten a high-fidelity speaker into its cabinet. 'It saves us a lot of time over the old method,' he was told. 'We used to use self-tapping screws, but this is much better. It cushions the speaker against vibration and also the screw used to crack the speaker cone; this can't happen with the tape.'

The salesman thanked the engineer and rushed off. That day he saw the other four factories which made audio equipment and made appointments with three of them for demonstrations of his tape. From then on, instead of opening his prospecting call by asking, 'Do you use tape?', he would say something like, 'We are specialists in products which are used in manufacturing processes. If I could have a quick look at your operation I might be able to suggest something which could save you time and money.'

There's nothing wrong with the rule which says that we should find out what people use and sell it to them, except that it locks us into their *present* way of doing things. How much more professional it is to show them a better way of doing something, and to sell them the product which allows them to do it! Not only will we gain their gratitude and respect, we shall effectively cut the opposition out of the running; they didn't demonstrate the better way, you did.

It's not easy to break this rule if you have been following it all your selling life. It's such a logical rule; of *course*, we should sell the customer what he uses. The example we looked at was in the industrial field, but the same thing applies in capital goods selling, in the consumer market – anywhere. How about the sale of time-share apartments? This is a relatively new business, and many people are not at all familiar with the concept of time-sharing. How far would the time-share salespeople get if they started the call by asking, 'Are you thinking of buying a time-share holiday home?' They would hardly get rich with that approach, because the answer would almost without exception be negative. No, they have to sell something to someone who doesn't use it and, and this is the point, who has never had any idea of using it.

This section has been about true creative selling, and as an advanced salesperson you have realised this long ago. Instead of following what has already been accepted, the salesperson who breaks the rule which says *sell him what he is using* is creating a sale where no sale existed. In many cases, this is the only way to make a sale.

Break the rule – sell him what he has no use for, what he has never bought before and has never dreamt of buying.

Chapter 6

SELLING ISN'T SERIOUS – LAUGH AT THE CUSTOMER!

First impressions are important. This is especially so in the case of a salesperson calling on a buyer, where the buyer is likely to be impressed by a serious, earnest, dedicated and committed attitude on the part of the salesperson. A salesperson is not a comedian and the selling process is no laughing matter.

Anybody want to argue with this rule? Impossible to deny that every word is true. Yet there are a few situations where taking it seriously can be the worst thing we can do. In this section we look at a few of these.

'I won't buy from you because . . .'
When we come up against any sort of sales resistance, it would seem that we have a serious situation, not something which we can get hilarious about. You are a salesperson and here are two reasons advanced by your customer for not buying from you:

'No. In the past your deliveries have been unreliable. I have twice had to keep my receiving depot open because your truck was late – you remember, I mentioned it to you before – and I can't keep doing it. There's nothing wrong with your products, but I don't have to live with the poor delivery situation I get from you, when my other supplier always delivers at the promised time.'

'No. I think that I had better stop buying from your company altogether. The word going round is that you people are going under, and I can't afford to commit myself to a supplier who is going to let me down without warning. That's the problem with you international people – you can pull out or close down your operation whenever it suits you. I'd rather deal with the local crowd, who will always be here when I need them.'

There you have two very different reasons for not buying. What is it, exactly, that makes them different? Several things. For one thing the first one has to do with something which happened in the past, while the second is a fear of something which might happen in the future. That isn't the important difference, though; what separates these two statements from each other is the fact that the first one is *true* while the second is *false*. We know that the first is true, because as the speaker said, he told you about one poor delivery when it had happened, and if he had been lying you would surely have taken him up on it. We can confidently take it that the second is false, since as a senior salesperson you would hardly continue to work for an outfit which was shortly going to close its doors.

There can be no argument about the way we treat the first of these statements; we treat it very seriously indeed. This customer has a genuine complaint and unless we treat it as such, we shall shortly have no customer. Exactly how we handle this problem has no place in these pages – whether to investigate the despatch system in our company, get our manager to bring it up at a management meeting, or wetnurse the delivery from our door to the customer's door – that is for circumstances themselves to decide. All we know is that the problem is a serious one and we are going to treat it seriously.

Ah, but the second statement? That's a very different affair. Here we have a rumour which is going around, perhaps planted by one of our less scrupulous competitors, and it is the sort of thing which can do indescribable damage to a company's reputation and to its sales. People won't deal with failures, or with companies who won't be around to provide service, parts or refills. They back off and buy from people they know will still be here tomorrow and in the year 2000.

What do we do? How do we scotch the rumour for all time and get the customer back on our books? As James Callaghan said, 'A lie can be halfway round the world before the truth has got its boots on.' This particular lie is a very serious one, but perhaps if we treat it seriously, we will leave the impression in the speaker's mind that we are really worried about it. 'I told the salesman what I'd heard about his company, and you should have seen his face drop. I suppose it must be true, after all.'

I didn't work out the best way to handle this, I'm merely copying what I heard a salesman say and what I saw him do in precisely this situation. The customer faced him with the charge: 'No matter what you say, the truth is that your company is about to close its operation in this country. That's the truth, isn't it?'

The salesman looked at the customer and for a moment his face was expressionless and his mouth was closed. No reaction at all. Then he laughed. He laughed loud and long. He squeezed up his eyes, he held his sides. The customer and I stared at him as though he had sprouted feathers. At last he took out a handkerchief and wiped his eyes. He said, 'Well, thank you; I haven't had a good laugh for ages. Well, let's get on with our business, shall we? Oh, by the way,' he said, as though it didn't really matter. 'As far as my company closing down is concerned, we have just bought twelve acres near Ipswich and we'll be building a twenty million pound research and development facility there. Doesn't sound much like a company which is on the way out.' He chuckled again, shaking his head. 'Now, about your stocks of the Princess model . . .'

He could have handled it in a serious way, of course; frowning earnestly, explaining the stake that the company had in the country and so forth. The trouble is that we have all heard people talk earnestly like that and vigorously denying that there is the slightest truth in the allegation. It can work, but don't we get the feeling that the speaker may be protesting too much? 'No smoke without fire' has ruined many reputations, personal and company.

So our salesman didn't bother to deny it. Instead he acted as though it were the funniest thing he had ever heard, and by doing so he simply laughed it out of court. Much more effective.

[36]

I had a similar experience when a confectionery manager accused a van salesman of selling cakes and doughnuts with artificial cream mixed into the real thing – a very serious allegation. The salesman stood in the shop and doubled up with laughter, until even the shop's customers stood and stared. When he had regained some of his composure, the salesman said, 'Oh, boy, Mr Maxey, if we started using that ersatz stuff there would be such a spate of sackings, from the managing director all the way down to the man who sweeps the bakehouse floor. Our whole reputation is based on the fact that we have never ever used anything but dairy products. No, sir; if I thought for a minute that there was anything in those cakes except flour and butter and eggs and milk and cream, I'd leave the country before my customers strung me up.' He gave the shop manager two cream cakes and said, 'There you are, Mr Maxey, take those home. I'm sure that your wife knows more about what genuine dairy products taste like than either of us. Ask her if she can taste anything artificial in those.' He went out to the van and came back carrying a tray of doughnuts. He laughed again. 'Wow – just wait until I tell our head baker what you said. He's half French, you know, and he gets pretty excitable. He'll probably drown himself in the milk vat.'

The thing which made it possible for both of these salesmen to laugh off the customer's objection was that in both cases the statements were completely untrue. This is the only time that laughter can be used. Where the problem is a real one, the objection is valid, the complaint is genuine, then of course we don't laugh. In that case, we take our coats off and get stuck in and handle the situation. But there are times when we dare not be serious, because by being serious it can easily look as though we are *worried*, and the only reason for us to be worried would be if the rumour, allegation, accusation or charge were true. By laughing at it, we show that it is ridiculous and we remove its sting.

I once did something quite appropriate in a similar situation. (Of course, we always remember those things which we did exactly right.) I was on my way to see an old and valued dealer of our company, and before I left my sales manager sat me down and explained things to me. He said, 'You don't know Monty, so let me fill you in. He is a very nice person, but he won't get it into his head that the price to him is the same as to all our other dealers. Now, he will pretend to expect that you will give him an extra two per cent on the disc ploughs and harrows. The thing is, don't whatever you do get into an argument with him on this, because he is an excitable little cuss and he tends to lose his temper. Then he will throw you out and write a long and furious letter to the board of directors, which doesn't impress them. The next day he is sorry, but by then the damage is done. Okay? On your way.'

Thanks very much, I thought. I'm on my way to see a volatile and valuable dealer, who will expect me to give him something which I'm not allowed to give him. If I don't give it to him, he will make the directors mad with me; if I do give it to him, it will make my boss mad with me. Talk about a 'no win' situation.

Mr Monty Syde was a charming gentleman. He offered me a choice of tea or sherry and we sipped tea and chatted of this and that. No business matters, just two gentlemen relaxing in the comfortable chairs in his office. At last we got round to business and I gave him our recommendations as to the equipment he should have in stock ready for the ploughing season. He made one or two minor changes and poured me another cup of tea while I made out the order. I handed it to him. He looked through it, smiled sadly and gave it back. 'Mr Beer, Peter Elston should have told you that as your oldest dealer, I get an extra two per cent on auxiliary equipment. If you will amend the order, I will be pleased to sign.'

Here it comes, I thought. What do I do to avoid an argument? There he sat, polite, smiling, perfectly at ease. I smiled back at him. I didn't feel like smiling, but I made myself do it. I made my mouth get broader and broader and I kept looking at him. I said, 'Mr Syde, Peter didn't only tell me that you were the oldest dealer; he also made it quite plain that you were the most valuable one in the whole country.'

For the first time he looked a little uncertain. 'The most valuable? But there are bigger dealers.'

I felt I had him now. 'Bigger, yes; so much bigger that you would think that they would be in line for extra discounts because of their bulk buying. They don't get it, of course; they pay the same as you. No, it's not the size of your dealership which makes you the most valuable, Mr Syde; it's the way you run your business, the quality of your service to the farmers, the pre-delivery preparation of the equipment, the high standard of your showroom.' There is a Russian saying that you can't spoil porridge by putting too much butter in it. I went on, and by now my smile was touching my ears. 'My goodness, if it was at all *possible* to give any dealer an extra two per cent, it would be you who got it, not those big dealers, even if they do sell as much as four times more than you do.' I handed him a pen. 'These new order pads don't need carbon paper; your signature comes through to the second copy without it.'

Mr Monty Syde stared at me as though he were trying to remember my face for future reference. He sighed, nodded, and slowly put the pen to the paper and signed. At last his smile came to match mine, and he put out his hand to shake mine.

The whole thing is that we don't laugh *at* the customer. Laugh at him and you could lose anything from your front teeth to your job. No, we are laughing at an accusation or suggestion which is simply not possible, and because it is not possible, it cannot be taken seriously.

You see why this book should never fall into the hands of an apprentice salesperson. Let him get the idea that laughter can be a useful tool in the sales interview, which we know is true, and he could end up in traction. Imagine a customer saying, 'Hey, the router you sold me broke down three times last week,' and the salesman doubling up as though he were listening to Spike Milligan, with horrific results.

As an advanced salesperson, you know where and when to be serious, and where and when to laugh. At the right time and place, laughter can work dramatically well. Know when to break the rule and it can get you out of situations as nothing else could.

Laugh at your boo-boos
I can't resist putting a tailpiece at the end of this section. It hasn't anything to do with what we've been talking about

here, except that it also has to do with laughter in a sales presentation, and it may help you out of an embarrassing situation.

In other writings, and also in my sales clinics, I have stressed the importance of being properly prepared for a physical demonstration of one's product or service. I have insisted again and again that the salesperson checks and double-checks that everything works, that the tank is full of diesel fuel, that the correct foot is on the sewing machine, that the voltage regulator is on 220 and not 110, that there is a full load of potatoes in the hopper, and that the teat is the right size for the bottle. I am sure that the people who attend my sales clinics think that I am a nit-picking fuss-budget about checking the demonstration equipment and, having done that, about rehearsing and practising and becoming so skilful at doing the demonstration that they could do it blindfold.

They may be right, but I make such a big thing of it because – and you know this as well as I do – in the sales demonstration Murphy's Law reigns supreme. If a thing can go wrong it does, and at the worst possible time. As an advanced salesperson, you are sitting back right now and looking into the past as you recall the horrible boo-boos you committed in the name of demonstrations. Remember? The day when the oh-so-strong material ripped in two when you put strain on it? What about the time when you opened the jar of cherries and ended up with maraschino all over your white blouse in front of fifty people? And of course, that disastrous business with the slide projector which blew its lamp in the middle of the audio-visual, and the box of spare lamps was empty.

We have all been victims, haven't we? That is, if we really are advanced salespeople. The bright young hopeful who said to the cricket captain, 'Put me in to bat early on, I've never made a duck,' received the reply, 'Then you can't have played very much cricket.' If you have never made a bad demonstration, then you haven't done very much selling.

Well, this book is not about how to demonstrate your products: that's for undergraduates, not for Masters of Selling. I put this codicil on to the end of this chapter because there is always the question: when we *do* chip the unbreakable crockery or try to use the photo-flash with a dead battery, what do we do next?

We can stand there looking embarrassed, of course. It's a fairly natural reaction; after all, we certainly are embarrassed. The trouble is that our audience, whether it consists of one person or an auditorium full of people, can also become embarrassed in empathy with us, and that is no way to run a successful demonstration.

I was demonstrating some of the properties of multigrade motor oil to a group of cartage contractors, and it was going well, with the group's attention at a high level. For one of the demonstrations, I had two test-tubes containing different grades of oil, each tube with a ball-bearing in it and each closed with a rubber stopper. The test, a very simple one, consisted of turning the test-tubes upside down to show the speed at which the ball-bearing sank in the oil – a rough sort of viscosity test. I held the test-tubes high above the lectern and upended them – and both stoppers came off and the oil and ball-bearings fell out on to the lectern, the oil splashing and the ball-bearings crashing all over the place. I was left standing with two empty test-tubes held on high and my shirt and trousers covered with oil.

What to do? I stared at the audience and they stared back at me. I saw just a twitch at the corner of someone's mouth and I started laughing. I stood there and laughed and they started laughing in their turn. We made such a noise that the manager of the conference centre came out of his office and looked in at the door. The thing is that if I had tried to keep it serious, it would have been an awful flop; by laughing my head off, I showed that it hadn't bothered me and therefore it shouldn't bother any of the audience.

Sometimes the best thing to do when you really make a mess of things is laugh it off; your listeners will realise that the boo-boo is not your normal way of doing things, and that you are enough of a professional not to be discomposed by it.

Chapter 7

DON'T SHOW THE CUSTOMER HOW IT WORKS

It's a rule so obvious that the sales training books don't even bother to stress it very much: the prospect deserves to know everything about the product before he buys. He has a right to know exactly how it works; if he doesn't, how can he possibly make an intelligent decision? So, show him how it works – better still, get him to work it himself, let him have all the time he needs to become adept at using the product. Then hit him with your closing technique, and get his signature on the order.

In short, show him how it works.

Difficult to argue with a basic rule like that, isn't it? Yet unless you break the rule, you can lose sales in a way that you may not believe possible.

We are, of course, talking about the demonstration aspect of the selling process. Now, any sales training worthy of the name will tell you that the demonstration is the most dramatic part of the sales presentation. We are told that this is the one part of the sales talk which the listener never forgets. He may forget the salesperson's name, the company he represents, the price of the product and the colours, sizes and weights that it comes in, but he will recall with crystal clarity that when he asked how strong the vacuum tube was the salesperson (who would have made Robert Morley look like an anorexic) put the tube on the ground *and stood on it*. Marvellous!

As we all know, the demonstration is the most powerful way of producing proof in the sales presentation. It creates, as nothing else can, the climate of *belief*. As an advanced salesperson, you have known this for years; you are convinced of the power of the demonstration, and – apart from the occasional catastrophe which we mentioned at the end of the last chapter – when you demonstrate, you do it with skill and enthusiasm.

As a sales trainer, I love watching demonstrations. I would crawl a mile over broken bottles to see a good demonstrator in action. Which is why, when I decided to put my old electric typewriter out to pasture and get a word-processor, I looked forward keenly to seeing some interesting demonstrations.

Three days later, having ventured forth into the roaring traffic's boom, I sat in the silence of my lonely room and wondered where the hell all the good demonstrators had gone, because although I was shown innumerable word-processors *I was not given one demonstration.*

Oh, I spent hours watching people filling screens with green words and pictures. I was invited to press keys myself (get the prospect involved, the sales courses tell us) and I dutifully did so. I was patiently and painstakingly taken through all the mysteries of word-processing. So why was I complaining? Did the salespeople not show me everything about the product? Yes, they did, and that was the trouble: instead of showing me why I should *buy* it, they showed me how it *worked*.

Right now, at this very moment, there are thousands of salespeople out there in front of a prospect, thinking that they are demonstrating a product, when what they are actually doing is instructing the prospect in the operation of that product.

Now the reaction to the above paragraph may be: 'But surely the buyer of a product has to know how to use that product?' Certainly, but let's get our priorities right. Here are two extracts from sales talks. Which would make you want to buy?

- 'This is the hexapoid button. Press it, wait three minutes for the fassenbrod barrier to warm up, and you are ready to enhance the gallipot effect.'

- 'Press this button and you will save yourself seven

minutes an hour. That's an extra hour a day, without it costing you a penny.'

Turn what could be the strongest part of the sale into an instruction session and you could turn your prospect away from your product forever.

Of *course* the buyer has to know how to operate it eventually, but you are engaged in a *sales* talk, not reading from the operator's manual.

Some time ago there appeared on TV a commercial for some gravy or other. Now we know that every second of TV commercial time costs a fortune, yet part of the script for this product went like this: 'You use boiling water, do you?' and the answer was: 'Oh, yes; the water must be boiling.' How to prepare it, not why we should buy it. We can very easily envisage the scenario that produced this fine piece of nonsense. The brand manager tells the advertising agency, 'This is a fine product, but unless the customer uses boiling water, it will be a mess.'

'No problem,' says the account executive. 'We'll make sure that people realise that.' And they waste priceless commercial time telling people how to *prepare* it. She has to use boiling water? Fine, so say it in large letters all over the packet, or put it on a card in the packet itself, so that she can't possibly miss it. Let her read about how to prepare it *once she has bought it*. Don't leave her with the feeling, after watching the commercial, that maybe after all she had better not buy the product, because there is obviously something rather tricky about getting it right; she had better stay with the product which she uses now. As it happens, she has to use boiling water for that one, too, but nobody frightened her off it by telling her how to use it.

The virus which causes this disease in salespeople is caught in product training sessions. Once it enters the body of the new salesperson, it is very difficult to eradicate, since the warm, friendly atmosphere of the training room is an ideal breeding ground for it. As far as internal training (as distinct from field training) is concerned, salespeople, as you are well aware, are developed in two separate ways: they are *taught* product knowledge and they are *trained* in selling skills.

Over-simplifying somewhat, the first tells them what to say, the second shows them how to say it. The product knowledge part usually comes before the selling skills part: the company teaches them about the product, before handing them over to someone like me to take them through the selling process. This is the logical way to go about it, and as a sales trainer I prefer it anyway – no good showing them how to fire the gun if they haven't been given any ammunition. However, this way – knowledge before skills – is the cause of much of the problem.

In the product knowledge section of his development, the trainee learns all about what he will be selling, and I do mean *all* about it – specifically, he learns how to use it. Obviously this is vital, because when he goes into the real world he will have to demonstrate it to people before they will buy. These courses are usually intensive and, depending on the industry, can be lengthy – as much as three months or more. When he comes off this course he is a knight-errant, the instruction manual is his Excalibur, and the damage is done. I try – all sales trainers try – to repair the damage, but often the virus has taken too strong a hold. He is going out there and he is going to show the prospective customer how the product works, even if it kills both of them. What it usually kills is the sale.

Once, in despair, I got a group of salesmen selling telephone answering machines to write a typical sales talk on a sheet of paper, then I got them to put the sheet in an envelope and give it to me. A week later I got the service manager of the company to take the group carefully through the routine of setting up the machine to operate correctly. I saw bewilderment and boredom on the faces around the room; they all knew how to do what they were being told by the service manager, since they had done it many times. When the service manager had left, I asked the top salesman to stand up and give us a brief but comprehensive sales talk on the machine, just as though he were selling it to a prospect. When he had done this, I asked the group if they could remember what the service manager had said and what their colleague had said. Yes, they could remember. I said, 'Will you please write down five differences between the two talks. Do it now.' I put a collated version of what they came up with on the board and it looked like this:

Service manager	Salesman
Longer	Shorter
Boring	Interesting
Very technical	Easily understandable
Mostly features	Mostly benefits
Told 'how to'	Showed 'why'

Then I gave them back the envelopes containing the sales talks which they had done the week before and asked them to read them silently. I said, 'Which does your talk look like – the explanation by a technical man or the presentation by a salesman?' They didn't have to answer; their faces showed that for the first time they understood the difference.

The customer must know how the product works, no question about it. If we sell him something without a thorough grounding in its operation, we are not doing our duty – and we risk having the product thrown back at us or getting continual complaints that it doesn't work properly. But while the office manager may *buy* the fax machine, he may not be the one who actually *uses* it. Therefore we give him the demonstration and we give Jerry, the junior clerk, the instruction session.

Show the customer how to use it? Sounds like a very good rule. But stick to it through thick and thin and there will be very much more thin than thick. This is a rule we cannot afford not to break.

Chapter 8

DON'T MAKE FRIENDS WITH THE CUSTOMER

The rule says, try to get onto a personal relationship with your customer, because when all else fails, the fact that you know him on a personal level can make the difference between making the sale and losing it, or keeping the business and watching the opposition take it away, perhaps because they have managed to get closer to the customer than you have – they are more friendly with him than you are. Naturally, the customer is more inclined to do business with someone he knows than with a comparative stranger.

An excellent rule. We can all think of customers, past and present, with whom we have enjoyed friendly relationships and to whom we have sold consistently well. There can't be any exception to this rule, can there? Ah, you say; this guy is warning us against trying to take advantage of our friendship with the customer, of implying – or even coming right out and saying – 'Hey, Chalkie, don't tell me you won't take an extra three cases, when we are such good pals!'

He insults our intelligence if he thinks that we would do anything so stupid, you say. No fear of that; we wouldn't push the customer to buy, just because we happen to sing in the church choir together.

I *don't* think that. I don't for a moment imagine that an advanced salesperson would use his friendship with a customer to push his products. My suggestion that we break the rule stems from an entirely different fear: I don't think that you may push your products too hard – *I think that you may stop selling them altogether.*

[47]

I try without much success to keep myself out of my writing, mainly because it is boring to read about the triumphs and disasters of one person. Also, since I have been working with salespeople all my business life, there are plenty of examples of other people which I can use. This chapter seems to be mostly about my own experiences, though, and I suppose it is because we are talking about an intensely personal part of the selling process – the relationship between the salesperson and the customer.

When I am working with a brand-new group of novice salespeople, I have no trouble with this subject. 'Get onto a level with the customer where you and he see each other as *people*,' I tell them. 'To him, you must be more than just the representative who sells him screwdrivers; to you, he must be more than just a signature at the bottom of the order. Get on the inside track with him.'

A good basic rule, and one which my new salespeople can easily grasp and appreciate. If they stay in the selling business, succeed in it and if, by chance, they end up back in a conference room with me ten years later, they might be forgiven for feeling that in the period since we last met I have developed softening of the brain. Now, after following my advice about getting on the inside track with the customer for the last ten years, they hear me say, 'Don't get too friendly with your customers!' I seem to have changed my tune.

I haven't really changed the tune, it's just that the words are different for different stages of experience in selling.

Actually, all I am doing is quoting the words of a sales manager of mine from years ago, who used to say to me, 'Are you sure you are not getting too friendly with the buyer at Town & Country?' I used to think he was crazy; how can you get too friendly with a customer? Certainly I was friendly with customers! I was a friendly sort of character and I made friends easily! (That was some time ago; these days I have a sort of reverence for the word 'friend' and I don't enter into friendships so casually.)

He wasn't crazy, as it happens; I *was* getting too friendly with my customers, as I found to my cost. We were about to launch a new octane-rated petrol, and I had to go round to all our dealers and tell them, very hush-hush, to run one of their underground tanks dry and to keep it dry for the great day. I called on my favourite dealer.

'Hi-de-hi, Robbie. Listen, I've got something very important to tell you. You have to – '

'Shut up, Michael.'

'No, Robbie, listen. You must – '

'Michael, I'm not in the mood. Sit down, yell for some coffee, drink it, and naff off.'

'Robbie, will you listen to me, mate?'

'No. N – O, no. Come back when I'm feeling better. Actually, don't bother to come back; I'll see you at the club next week and you can tell me whatever it is you want to get off your chest on Tuesday night.' -

'Robbie – '

'NO!'

Yes, it happened, just as I have put it down here. I had become so friendly with my customer that he could *refuse* to listen to me. If you had thought that I was warning against friendliness because of a salesperson using it to force a sale, here is the answer; the danger is that the customer can use the relationship to block the sales presentation. In the case above, my friend, the customer, used our relationship to throw me out. How do you like that? Robbie was not by nature a rude, brusque or mannerless personality, but he knew that he could get away with that sort of behaviour *because we were friends*. Had I been a stranger, he would never have acted in that way. Had I been on professional, business terms with him he would have listened to me – simple good manners would have dictated thus.

Certainly the customer/salesperson relationship is important and only an idiot would think otherwise, but what *sort* of relationship should it be? In a few words, it can be as close as you like – but it is always and forever a *professional* relationship, and my mistake was in allowing it to deteriorate (yes, the word is deliberate) into a *social* relationship.

Friendly? Of course we can be friendly. I have clients who have used my training services for many years and with whom I have friendly relationships which I value immensely, and which have been very profitable to me and, I hope, to them too. I call many of them by their first names and when I visit

[49]

them to discuss training, the meeting is relaxed and informal. However, I have learnt by bitter experience never to forget why we are talking to each other. Friendly the atmosphere may be, by all means, but what we are engaged in *is not a social call*. If it were not for business, I would not be there; therefore I cannot forget for one instant that it is a business call. He may pull my leg about my favourite rugby team's terrible record, I can tell him that the coffee he forces me to drink is the world's worst, we can call each other 'Tim' and 'Michael', but when the pleasantries have been exchanged, I must be able to give a proper sales presentation, and I can't do that on a social call.

Look at it another way: suppose you are handed a new product which you have to put on the market. It is a good product, but it needs a full, formal sales presentation and demonstration in order to sell it. You can expect some fairly strong sales resistance and some stiff opposition from competitive products. You have fifty prospects lined up, ready to hear your sales talk. Think, now; would you rather those fifty people were perfect strangers, or close friends? Most of us would take the strangers, thanks.

Am I getting through to you on this? Perhaps you are saying, 'Well, he can give all the examples he likes, but I am very friendly with my customers, and a hell of a lot of business comes to me through those friendships.'

I don't doubt you for a moment; in fact, I say the same thing. Only last week a valued client phoned me and gave me the name of a company executive. 'Phone him, Mr Beer; he's expecting your call. I told him that you gave the keynote speech at our annual conference and that it set the right tone for the whole meeting.' Now, you and I know that this sort of relationship is priceless and that it can make a tremendous difference to your sales volume. But did you notice something about that phone call? He called me 'Mr Beer'. We are not even on first-name terms, he and I.

The whole business of first or last names, whether you call your customer 'Ms North' or 'Martha', or 'Mr South' or 'Arthur', depends very much on what sort of people they are and what sort of person you are. I once worked with a partner, a big, friendly bear of a man, jovial, hail-fellow-well-met to everyone. He had the sort of personality which had the effect

[50]

that five minutes after he walked into a room, all the women were in love with him and all the men wanted to lend him money. He was a better salesman than me, and I say it without resentment; not because of his personality, he just was. Now we had a client who had bought from us but only in a small way, and we could see that there was tremendous potential for more business from him. It happened that this client had met my partner socially, outside business, and I had not. He was on first-name terms with my partner (let's face it, even the traffic police were on first-name terms with him) and I was not. But when the time came to sell this man more of our services, my partner tried, and failed. 'I couldn't seem to get through to him, Michael. Had a very good meeting with him, but no dice.' I left it for a month, and then walked in on the man and sold him the whole package we had suggested. All right, circumstances may have changed for him in the interval, or my partner's call could have softened him up for my sale; you can't step into the same river twice. The point is that the social relationship failed and the professional relationship succeeded, as it so often does.

I went out with the area manager of a company selling timber products. 'Should be an interesting call, this one,' he said. 'This is a builder who buys his wooden doors from his brother-in-law.' I thought, wow; anyone who could call a sales call like that 'interesting' would describe World War II as a squabble. Well, as it happened, it *was* interesting. The prospect received us without very much warmth or friendliness, explaining that he bought most of his doors from 'another supplier' and he was satisfied with the service he received from them. The area manager went ahead with his presentation and got across one or two points that made the prospect frown. 'My broth – That is, my present supplier, has never mentioned that to me,' he grumbled. 'Why, that could save my carpenters a lot of time!' We walked out of there with signed orders for three-quarters of his door business. He said, almost apologetically, 'There are private reasons why I can't give you all my door business.' I thought, 'Right; your wife will kill you when her brother comes crying to her.'

It would be easy to blame that man's brother-in-law for not doing a decent selling job on him, but he was severely handicapped by being too close socially to his customer.

Finally, the most awful example of all. Frankly, I hesitated to put this one on paper because although it was a long time ago, the memory still rankles. It is the ultimate example of what can happen when you get too friendly with your customer.

I sold oil to industrial users, as distinct from service stations, and one of my favourite and most valued customers was Uncle Ben, a dam-building contractor. Everyone called him Uncle Ben – lovely person, he was. I was young and green and it was a great source of pride to me that I had managed to get all of Uncle Ben's oil business; he was one hundred per cent mine. I had a warm and close relationship with him, and with his wife who always gave me lunch if I happened to call in the middle of the day, and who used to nag me about not dressing warmly enough. I used to do a little bragging around the company sales meetings: 'You guys should have customers as loyal as Uncle Ben.'

Then one grey day I drove into Uncle Ben's yard and all I could see were piles of opposition oil drums. What a sight – I had never realised what a nasty combination of colours red and yellow produced. In a panic I sought out my loyal customer.

'Er – Uncle Ben; those drums out there. That's a mistake, I suppose? They sent them to the wrong address, huh?'

Uncle Ben said in his slow way, 'No, Michael, it's no mistake. I ordered that oil.'

'But why?'

'Well, the salesman explained just what a wonderful oil it is.'

'But – ' I couldn't believe this was happening. 'How do you mean, a wonderful oil?'

'Well,' Uncle Ben frowned, trying to remember. 'He told me that this oil has a – what's its name? A rust and corrosion inhibitor, that's it. You see, Michael, when I put my back-hoes and payloaders away for the winter, that stuff protects the insides of the engines.'

'But my oil has a R and C inhibitor in it, too!'

'Ah, but he also said that his oil has a – ' he hesitated. 'An anti-foaming agent. It's like a little bloke sitting in the oil and he has a little pin to prick the bubbles which form, so the oil film stays unbroken and gives perfect protection to the moving parts.'

Frantic now, I said, 'But the oil that I sell you – sold you – also has an anti-foamer. Uncle Ben, it has all the additives in it that this oil has!'

He looked at me in surprise. 'But Michael, why didn't you ever tell me, then?'

Now in fact, he was wrong. I *had* told him. I had explained all about all the additives and what each one of them did. The trouble was that I had explained all that *eighteen months ago*, and Uncle Ben had simply forgotten. People do forget, you know. They are persuaded to buy a product by listening to and understanding a sound, professional sales presentation. Good, they think. This product has the things which will give me what I want from such a product. They buy the product and they go on using it and buying more of it, but as time goes by, while they are still happy with the product and what it is doing for them, they have forgotten just what it was that made them buy it in the first place.

Uncle Ben had forgotten why he first bought my oil, but I didn't care, because now he was buying from me, not because of the product, but because of the close personal relationship which had formed between us. Why should he think of dealing with someone else? His wife would pack some of her tipsy tart for me to take home; did that sound like someone who would change to another supplier?

Then along comes the opposition salesman, so smooth that he can slide uphill, and gives my loyal customer the same sales talk that I gave him eighteen months ago – and steals him away from me. The same way, come to think of it, that I stole him away from his previous supplier.

There's the real danger. We get so cosy with our customers that we forget that we have to keep selling to them *the products which they are already buying from us*. People need to be reminded just why they are buying the things which they are using; they need to be reassured that the products are still doing for them the things which made them buy at the beginning.

Not only that; they need to realise that the product is still the best that money can buy, and I'll prove this important point to you right now, without your having to move from your chair. Suppose that you have an electric razor, or a steam iron, say. You have been using it for about a year and you are very happy with it; it does just what you hoped it would do when you bought it. Now you open a magazine or newspaper and there is a big advertisement for the exact model of razor or iron which you own. What do you do? You know very well what you do; you read the advertisement from top to bottom, every word of it. Why? So that you can be reassured that what you are using is still the best available. *You resell yourself on the product*.

Why should I have given Uncle Ben another sales talk on the product when he liked it and liked me? Because he needed reassuring about it. This doesn't mean, of course, that we have to give our regular customers a full sales presentation every time we see them; they would think we had gone bonkers. But it does mean that every now and then we have to remind them why they bought it in the first place, and what it is still doing for them. 'Now that winter's coming on, Uncle Ben, it's comforting to know that your plant will be protected in storage . . . ' Or, 'Look at these two pictures, Uncle Ben. In this one the oil is just oil. See how the foaming is destroying the oil film? This one has our defoamer in it. See? Not a single bubble. Please, Aunt Mary, not another slice or I'll burst. Oh, well, just a small one, then.'

Get on friendly terms with our customers? Of course we can. But let's be very careful that we don't let the precious *professional* customer/salesperson relationship degenerate into a purely *social* one. As an advanced salesperson, you will know through your own experience that you can move from a formal approach and atmosphere to a more relaxed and informal one, but that it is completely impossible to move the other way. Once you have allowed yourself to become *too* friendly, you lose the ability to sell assertively to that customer – and there is no way back.

Chapter 9

YOU ARE NOT ON THE CUSTOMER'S SIDE

The rule is that we get on the customer's side of the desk (or counter or machine) as quickly as possible; that is to say, as quickly as possible we show him that when it comes to our products, our service, our back-up, our deliveries and the whole package which makes up the customer/supplier business, we are working with him as closely as fleas on a dog. We want him to realise that we *belong* to him; that we are not the sort of company which loses interest in him the moment he signs the order, then keeps its distance until the time comes for him to sign another one. As a customer, he has a right to feel that we are on his side.

This sounds like an excellent rule and one which should definitely get us on the inside track with the customer. A good rule and an obvious one, it would seem; do we even need to discuss it? Not only do we have to discuss it, but if we wish to be thought of as advanced salespeople, we shall in certain situations have to break it mercilessly.

I was moving house from one city to another, and everything that could possibly go wrong went wrong, along with a few things that couldn't possibly go wrong. Most of these things were the direct fault of the van lines company which was doing the moving, and when I was finally confronted with a particularly stupid aspect of their operation, I muttered to the supervisor, 'You work for a bloody awful company, my friend.'

Well, I must have been badly provoked to say something like that, because I don't usually let my bad temper show to

[55]

subordinates for something that is the fault of their superiors. I didn't know what reaction to expect from this man, but what he said took me completely by surprise. He threw the clipboard he was holding onto the floor and said, 'You think I work for a bloody awful company? Listen, you don't know half of it. Let *me* tell *you* what a (expletives deleted) company I work for!' Off he went, telling me in purple prose just how awful it was. He showed a fluent, if primitive, command of language and he did not repeat himself once.

Now, this is an extreme case, but it has always stuck in my mind. What this supervisor did was get right on my side. He agreed with me about the deficiencies of his company in every detail I could think of and several which hadn't occurred to me. He and I were of one mind about what, in both our opinions, was one of the worst van lines in the world.

A hundred years later – it was only the evening of the same day, it merely seemed that a century had passed – I was sitting on a carton in my new living-room with a life-saving drink and thinking about my new-found ally, the mutinous supervisor. One would think that I saw him as someone I could rely on, my only friend in a company which didn't care about me, the customer. I didn't think of him in that way at all. I saw him as a misfit, someone who didn't deserve to hold down any sort of responsible job and furthermore, a particularly stupid person who didn't have the sense to leave a company which he hated.

And this is where we break the rule, you see. We must certainly get close to the customer; we must see to his wants and needs, handle his complaints and problems, making sure that he gets what he deserves as a valued buyer of our products. But when the storm clouds gather, when he tells you what terrible service he is getting, how badly he was treated by your switchboard operator, how many times your order department has got things wrong, that your credit manager is a dreamer and your engineer an idiot – then the advanced salesperson knows exactly where he stands, and it is not on the side of the customer against his own company. Compare these two answers to a customer who has a grievance – a genuine one, mind you – against a company:

'Oh, Mr Henderson, don't tell me that bunch of clowns in Despatch has got another delivery wrong! That's the third time this month! I don't know why we don't fire the whole lot of them. Don't worry, sir; when I get back to the office a few heads are going to roll. I'll show them that they can't treat my customers like this.'

'Mr Henderson, I can understand how you feel, getting your goods two days late and then part of the order being wrong. I know that Dan Cornwell, the Despatch manager, will be particularly unhappy about it; he and his team are proud of their record of promptness and accuracy. They are a really hard-working bunch, too. Never mind, I'll straighten it out as soon as I get back to the office and you'll have the right stuff this afternoon – probably with a phone call from Dan, apologising.'

In both of those cases, the salesman showed his dismay at the poor service and his intention of doing something about it right away. The difference? In the first example, he got on the customer's side against the company; in the second, he, as it were, reached over to help the customer, *but he stayed on the company's side.*

The whole point here is that when the van lines supervisor came over to my side against his company, I didn't think the more of him; I didn't admire him, or see him as a new bosom pal; my feeling was very simple – I despised him.

Your customer is not a moron. Your customer knows who employs you, who pays your salary. Your customer admires you only when, in the face of grumbles, complaints, criticisms and accusations – usually about something which is not your fault – you stand there and take it. You don't blame other people or departments in your own company: 'Hey, Mr Henderson, take it easy on me, will you? I don't *make* the damn things, I just sell them!' You realise, as all advanced salespeople realise, that part of your job is to be a whipping boy for the whole organisation, from the chief executive all the way down to the man who carries the product from the delivery van into the customer's receiving bays and drops it on the store-man's foot. Anything that goes wrong between the company and the customer is going to be dumped at your door.

Fair? Now why on earth should it be fair? Go back and read

the small print and see where it clearly states: *whereas the aforementioned individual has willingly and without coercion decided to become a* **salesperson,** *with all the advantages and privileges of that exalted position,* **be it known** *that if a truck breaks down* **or if** *a clerk sends the customer a rude letter* **or if** *the said customer overloads the product until it breaks,* **it shall be reckoned and assumed** *that all these occurrences shall be the direct and non-transferable fault of the aforesaid* **salesperson,** *who shall unreservedly accept the blame for all such occurrences, past, present and to come.*

You know that, you have always known and accepted it; it goes with the luxury car, the enormous salary, the unlimited expense account, the slush fund and the colossal bonus which all salespeople enjoy.

When it comes to knowledge of a customer's needs, his buying habits, his attitude, his likes and dislikes, we get as close to him as his identical twin, but we never get 'on his side'.

It would be nice to think that there *are* no 'sides', that we are all one happy family, our customers and our company. When things are humming along merrily with no problems and no complaints, it does no harm to think so, even though it isn't true; but when things go wrong, we are suddenly faced with the truth, and the truth is that there *are* two sides, the customer's and the company's, and the advanced salesperson is never in the slightest doubt as to which he is on. This doesn't mean that we are against the customer; we don't have to be *against* anyone. What it does mean is that we are – first, last and always – *for* the company whose business card we carry.

Go over to your customer's side the moment a problem arises and you will find that nobody loves a renegade. He is despised both by the side he leaves and the side he joins.

'Get on the customer's side' is a rule we *must* break if we are to retain the confidence of our company, the goodwill of the customer – and our own self-respect.

Chapter 10

SOFT SELL IS OUT – HARD SELL RULES, OKAY!

There is one rule which we don't break under any circumstances whatever and that is the one that says: No high-pressure selling! But let's make sure that we know what we are talking about here. There are many definitions of high-pressure selling, and some of them are wrong. No doubt, as a salesperson who has been around for some time, you will have your own definition, but you might be interested in mine so that you can compare it with yours. Mine goes like this: high-pressure selling is selling where the customer doesn't need it, where he can't afford it, or where the salesperson is guilty of overstepping the bounds of good manners and taste. If you sell a lawnmower to a person in a high-rise flat, or a gold watch to someone who is behind with his rent, or if they show you out of the door and you jump back in through the window – all of that is high-pressure selling and is unacceptable, no exceptions, no discussion needed.

But what about hard sell? Ah, that is another thing entirely. Here is a rule which I followed religiously for the early part of my selling life; it was my credo, repeated to myself before every sales presentation: 'I am a soft-sell salesman. I allow the customer to make the decision. I do not presume to dictate to him how he should spend his money. Hard-sell salesmen are a lot of uncouth yobbos who walk on their knuckles, and I would die rather than be counted with them.'

All very right and proper, and with an attitude like that any salesperson can put his head on his pillow with a clear conscience. If he can afford a pillow, that is, because he certainly isn't making very much money.

This attitude is astonishingly common among new salespeople, and the reason is an interesting one. It has to do with exactly how they got into selling in the first place. Now I don't know what the circumstances were that put you into the selling business, but I don't imagine that as a bright-eyed teenager you said to your parents, 'When I grow up I'm going to sell concrete-hardening additives to the construction industry.' If you were like most of the rest of us, you became a salesperson because you couldn't afford to go to university, or because unemployment was high when you left school and jobs were scarce, or simply because you wanted to start earning reasonable money early on without a long apprenticeship.

However it was, for many people the fact that they were in selling was a rather nasty shock – they didn't *want* it. There were plenty of other things they would rather have done, they simply couldn't do them for one reason or another. Their reaction, then, was something like mine: 'Soft sell, always soft sell, never hard sell; then at least nobody can call you a high pressure salesperson.'

The big mistake here, apart from the awful negative attitude, is of course equating hard sell with high pressure. We'll get to that in a moment, but first, let's articulate the rule by which so many salespeople run their selling lives:

The days of the hard-sell salesman are gone, thank heaven. The sleazy character who wore you down with his high-power sales talk, who pushed you into buying, is as dead as yesterday's headlines. The name of the game these days is soft sell. We show him the product, we tell him exactly what it will do for him, answer all his questions, and make the proposal. Soft sell means that we will always be welcome, that the customer's door will always be open for the next call. Soft sell means conversational selling – no badgering or bullying him into buying. Let him make his own decision!

The trouble is that the rule sounds so logical, quite apart from the fact that it also sounds like plain, common, good manners. Any lady or gentleman salesperson would be happy to accept it as part of a personal ethical code. The brutal truth is that they would probably be *unemployed* salespeople, because with that sort of attitude they would not be bringing in very impressive sales figures, and the chance of holding down a job in any sort of competitive selling situation would not be bright.

No, I'm afraid that we shall have to break that rule if we intend to make anything like a decent living in selling. You are an advanced salesperson and that means that you have broken it many times. You may not have realised that you have broken it, but you did, every time you changed your customer from the first quote to the second:

'Sorry, but I'm perfectly happy with what I have now. I see no reason to change.'

'You know, what you say makes a lot of sense. I have never thought of it in that way before.'

What happened between the first quote and the second? What happened was that you *changed his mind*. After a flat turn-down, you got him on to your side. You don't do that with soft sell, you know; that's a hard-sell situation.

Time to define hard sell. Again, you will have your own definition but you might be interested in mine: hard sell is knowing, without any doubt or reservation, that the customer needs the product, that it will really do what he wants it to do, and that he can afford to buy it – *and then going hard for the sale*. That's it.

You may care to read that definition again and then go back to the definition of high pressure, and it will immediately become evident that there is all the difference in the world between the two. This difference is most easily seen in the two words *need* and *afford*. In high-pressure selling, they don't need it and/or they can't afford it; in hard sell, they do need it and they can afford it. Once the latter situation has been established, the advanced salesperson gives it all he's got in order to get the order signed.

It took me some time to change my personal selling philosophy from the sublime nonsense of my early years in selling to the creed which I have held unchanged since then, but once I did I became a more effective salesman overnight. My new outlook is much shorter and simpler than the old one and it goes like this: *easy sell in easy times – hard sell in hard times*. The easy times in selling are over for good. The days when you could pick up a couple of lines, spread your wares in front of the customer and wait, pen poised over the order form while he decided how much of this and how much of that – those days are gone the way of the dickey-seat and the crystal set. We are now in hard times in selling. This does not mean hard in the sense of being deprived, or living in the depression years all over again, but hard in that we are in a never-ending fight for the customer's pounds and pence against strong, go-ahead, well-organised competitive companies, who are selling fine products with good back-up service and state-of-the-art promotion campaigns. The advanced salesperson doesn't mind this; he expects and even revels in the cut and thrust – but he knows very well that when you are fighting an opponent who is using a flame-thrower, you don't win with a catapult.

Here is easy sell:

'Yes, your display stands look very nice, but the trouble is that the stands I'm using are only eighteen months old and they are as good as new. Why, in my books they are written down only thirty per cent. On that basis, I have to keep using them for at least another three years before I can think of getting rid of them.'

'Yes, I can see your point. Well, I'll be around in three years' time to sell you some really good stands. Thank you for listening to my presentation, anyway.'

'You're very welcome; come back any time.'

That was easy sell; waste of a call, waste of half an hour, waste of an opportunity.

In answer to the same put-off from the same customer, this is hard sell:

'In your books they may be standing you in at seventy per cent of their original cost, but that is figures on a piece of paper; in the real world, they are costing you a fortune. Stand outside your shop and compare your window display with those of the other five shops in this part of the complex. You can see that those outdated stands are chasing customers across the street into the opposition. Your windows look awful, and it's not your fault; you are performing near-miracles with those stands, but it isn't enough. What you have to do is take a deep breath and put your accountant into shock by throwing out the stands, selling them for whatever you can get, no matter how low it is – and start pulling customers into the shop with the sort of display I have just shown you. Do it, Mr Kilby; every day you delay is costing you money.'

That is, of course, only a small extract of a sales presentation, but how do you feel about it? Perhaps you are saying to yourself, 'That's high-pressure selling. Much too pushy, knocks the opposition product, won't let the customer make up his own mind. No matter what he may call it, I call it high-pressure.' If you feel like that, then I have done a bad job of communication so far in this chapter. Would you please go back to the beginning and read it again? I'd appreciate it.

Now that you have had a second look at it, perhaps it is easier to see that while the second example might not have been the ultimate in diplomacy and tact, it did at least fit into the definition of hard sell and did not, as far as we can tell, fit into the definition of high pressure.

If I ever did a favour for an angel and I was given one wish, I would wish for the eloquence to get into the heads of my selling skills groups the difference between *aggressive* selling and *assertive* selling. The dictionary in the woolly headed way of most dictionaries has the two words as synonyms for each other, at least as third or fourth definitions, but this is nonsense. 'Aggressive' comes straight from the Medieval Latin word *aggressare*, 'to attack'. Well, you don't attack your customer, not even verbally. 'Assertive' comes from the verb 'assert' which means 'to insist on, to state categorically'. Exactly so. Aggressive selling is high pressure and therefore unacceptable; assertive selling is hard sell and therefore essential to our success.

[63]

When our tumble-drier gave up the ghost, my wife made a list of the stores near us which sold appliances. She came home, having bought from the very last store on the list. I said, 'Did you start at the bottom of the list, or didn't the other stores have any tumble-driers in stock?'

She said, 'No, I started at the top of the list, and they all had what I wanted in stock. It was just that the last store on the list was the only one which seemed to want to sell me a tumble-drier today.'

If you are still afraid of hard sell, then hear me; people *want* to be sold! The novice salesperson, imbued with the idea that he must exhibit reserve and deference, and avoid like the plague any hint of pushiness, loses sight of the fact that the decision to buy is a two-way thing; you, the salesperson, decide on the basis of your knowledge and experience that yes, this is the exact product the customer needs, so sell it to her; she, the customer, decides on the basis of her knowledge and experience that yes, as you have described and demonstrated the product, it is indeed the exact product she needs, so she buys it. Why shouldn't the salesperson also be involved in that decision? Let's help the customer by making half the decision for her, so that the other half, the part she makes herself, is easier for her.

Break the soft-sell rule. If you have really done your homework on the two questions – does he really need it? Can he really afford it? – you will be doing the customer a real service with your hard sell.

Chapter 11
————————————

DON'T LET HIM BUY

The rule, and I have stated it hundreds of times to thousands of salespeople, is simple: every call is a sales call. There is no such thing as a 'courtesy' call. There is no such thing as a 'contact' call. Every call made by a salesperson has as its aim either a sale made then and there, or a definite progress towards a sale in the future. We are *always* trying to sell. We must *never* miss an opportunity of selling.

I do my very best to get this rule into the heads of my new salespeople, so if you have ever attended one of my selling skills clinics, you may wonder how I can possibly make an about-turn and suggest that you break it.

It's still an axiom of good salesmanship, and we break it only on special occasions. Break it we must, though, when the need arises. Let's look at a few examples of the need. We shall see that there are times when we shouldn't try to sell, and you are probably aware of some of these already. But has it occurred to you that there are times when we should absolutely *refuse* to sell? Let's see.

I went out with a senior salesman to call on the branch of a supermarket. He sold tea and coffee, and the situation was that the branch had just had a change of managers. The salesman wanted to meet the new manager, welcome him to the area and, if at all possible, take an order from him.

We met the man and he proved to be pleasant and approachable. As it happened, he had been transferred to this branch from a smaller one in a much lower-income part of town; the branch he now managed served several luxury suburbs. He agreed that he needed more stock, and he and the salesman sat down to make up an order. He said, 'I see that my predecessor didn't buy your very popular four-ounce packet of tea. You'd better send me six cases of it.'

The salesman said, 'He didn't buy it from us because it doesn't sell; not in this part of the world, anyway.'

'Oh, nonsense,' the manager said. 'Really good, fast-moving line. Six cases, please.'

The salesman looked uncomfortable. 'I really must advise against it. My experience – '

'*Your* experience? My friend, I'm a good deal older than you and it's *my* experience I rely on. Do you think I don't know this business backwards and forwards?' He tapped his desk impatiently. 'Come on, come on; do I have to fight you to get you to sell it to me?'

We walked out of there with an order which included six cases of the four-ounce pack. The salesman shook his head. 'Damn it all, he doesn't seem to realise that he isn't still in his old branch. The four-ouncer *is* a good seller there, but his new customers don't buy tea in that sort of pack.' He shrugged his shoulders. 'Hell, I don't know – perhaps he does know his business better than I do.'

A few months later he phoned me. He said, 'Do you remember when I didn't want to sell the manager of the Buy-Rite branch that four-ounce pack of tea?'

I said, 'Yes, I do. Was he right? Has he sold it out and re-ordered?'

The salesman said explosively, 'He was as wrong as it is possible to be. Not only has he not sold any of the product, he now wants to return the whole six cases for full credit, and worst of all, he blames me for selling it to him!'

'But you advised him not to buy; I was there when you did it!'

'I know, I know. I reminded him that I was against the sale. Know what he said? "You should have refused to sell it to me!" '

You are an advanced salesperson, so don't tell me that you haven't been through an experience similar to this. Isn't it astonishing how a customer's mind can work? Sell him a product which does a good job for him and he says, 'That was a good decision of mine, to buy that.' Let him buy something which turns out to be wrong for him, and it is suddenly: 'That idiot of a salesman sold me a pup.'

Yes, I see you there in the back row, shaking your head. I hear you saying, 'That's all very well, but there are times when you can't actually and literally refuse to sell a product to someone, even when you know it isn't the right thing for him. He wants it, he is determined to have it, and he threatens, if you won't sell it to him, to go to the opposition and buy it from them. Then what?'

Good point. What do we do? Well, it certainly isn't part of our contract with the company we represent that we should chase potential customers across the street into the welcoming arms of the opposition. They will probably be delighted to take his order and his money – and he will *still* have bought the wrong product. You might like to try something which I have done more than once; it used to produce interesting reactions from customers who were determined to buy what I sold, no matter what I felt about it.

This particular case concerned a customer who wanted to buy a bulldozer, and here I have to get a little technical. We call them all 'bulldozers' but in fact there is the simple bulldozer itself, which can push earth only in a straight line, directly forward, and then there is the 'angledozer' which has a blade which can be angled to either side so as to throw the soil to one side or the other – useful for grading, and jobs like that.

Now, this customer told me that all he wanted was the straight-blade bulldozer. 'I shan't be doing any grading with it,' he said. My heart sank into my boots, because I had played this scene before with other actors, and I knew the script by heart.

I said, 'I know that it may seem as if you don't need the angling facility, but circumstances change, and you won't like it when you suddenly get a call for a grading job and all you have is the straight-blade machine.'

I won't put it all down, but it ended, as I knew it would, with him saying, 'Look, are you going to sell me what I want or do I get it from someone else?'

I took a deep breath and said, 'Sir, I'll sell you the straight-blade dozer. When we deliver it, I am going to be there in person, and when you sign the delivery note I am going to give you a letter which will state that I advised you against taking the straight-blade model, but that you insisted on it.' I said, 'You see, when you come back and complain to my boss that I sold you the wrong product, I simply must have the copy of that letter on file to protect myself.'

He looked at me for what seemed like a long time. 'You are really serious about this, aren't you?'

I said, 'I have to be. This machine is costing you a fortune, and you are going to be furious when you realise that it won't do what you want it to do. I'm just trying to make sure that you're not furious with *me*.'

He looked irritated. 'Oh, for God's sake make it the angledozer then, if you're going to go on and on about it.'

It wasn't three months after he took delivery of the unit that he phoned me and said, 'Next time you are out this way, pop in.' I went to see him the next week, and lo and behold, there was the machine with its blade angled, doing a lovely job of grading the wall of an earth dam. He said, 'I thought you would like to see the unit at work. I'm big enough to apologise, and thank you for not letting me buy the straight-blade model.'

Try this the next time a customer throws the ultimatum at you: sell it to me or I buy the opposition. Tell him why you advise against it, and say that when you deliver it, you will also be delivering a letter disclaiming responsibility. It makes him sit back and think – and it does your stature as an advanced salesperson no harm at all in his eyes. He will think: here is someone who, far from flogging me anything he can offload, actually won't take my money, because he honestly believes it is the wrong thing for me. I have had a customer phone my boss and congratulate him on having an honest salesman on his team!

The next example of calling without a thought of selling may never apply to you. I hope it never does, because it is the sort of thing which wakes sales managers screaming in the night. We had a salesman who didn't do much to enhance his company's image in his territory; to give you a hint, he was cited as co-respondent in the messy divorce of one of our more valuable customers. Well, after we had fired him so fast that he had no time to close the door behind him, we had no

[68]

salesman to put into his territory, so we lost out in two ways: first, by our ex-salesman giving a completely new dimension to the term 'customer service', and then by the fact that for nearly two months we had no salesman there at all.

As you can imagine, our sales in that territory went down like a rock in a pond. When we finally did put a new salesman in there – and he *was* new; it was his first time in the field – the poor bloke thought he had fallen into a meat grinder. Not only did he not get a single sale in the first week, but he learnt several new words which don't appear in the dictionary.

We realised that we had been stupid to throw him to the wolves and we said, 'All right. First, we are taking your quota away. You have no sales target to reach because it wouldn't mean anything; no matter how small we made it, you probably wouldn't make it. Second, I am coming out with you and we are going to call on every single one of your customers.'

'What are we going to tell them?'

'We are going to tell them that we are not going to sell them anything.'

This didn't make sense to the new boy, but he did look relieved that he apparently wasn't going to face the music by himself. It was no fun. We called on every one of his hundred and fifty-odd customers and I gave the same speech to each one. I started off by saying, 'We are not here to sell you anything.' In most cases the reply to this was something like, 'Damn right,' or 'That's just as well,' or 'Good, because I'm not buying anything from you.' Just the sort of encouraging responses every salesperson hopes for.

I went on, 'We don't deserve your business. In your place, I would feel exactly the same as you. I've come here to introduce Charlie Newman; this is his territory. Now, I'm not asking you to buy five pence worth of product from Charlie, but this is now his beat, so may he just put his head around your door once a month? He won't waste your time and he certainly won't ask you to buy. But as you know, we are the innovators in the industry, and we often have new ideas to save people time and money. If Charlie has something new to show you, will you at least listen to him for five minutes?'

Hardly a high-powered sales talk, but what else could I say? I had to get Charlie inside somehow. Well, most of them said all right, send him round and he can have his five minutes a month. Our company seemed still to retain some shreds of our former reputation, even though we had done our best to destroy it.

It was a long, slow process. Charlie kept rigidly to our agreed five minutes on each call. He didn't carry a briefcase or anything in his hands at all, but every now and then he would have some leaflets of a new product in his pocket, or a comparison test, or a copy of a letter from a satisfied customer – that sort of thing. Charlie was an endearing sort of character, and the customers got to like him, even if they still had serious reservations about us as a company. It got to be quite a joke with some of them that he never took more than five minutes and he didn't ever ask for their business.

Slowly, slowly, the orders started coming. Charlie would stand up to go after his five minutes and the customer would say something like, 'Do you still make that airweight onion-skin in yellow?' Charlie would go into shock and manage a nod. 'Let me have ten reams, will you?' And an old customer was back in the fold. It took the best part of a year before it made sense to give him a sales target again, and he did it *by not trying to sell anything*. Had we gone back into that territory with a senior, hotshot salesman and a smooth line of talk, doing our best to sell, I think we would have committed sales suicide.

If – not if, when, since every company has disasters of some sort – your company has done something so terrible that customers have been chased away, the natural impulse is to chase after them. Don't do it. Try telling them that you know that you don't deserve their business, but may you keep calling, since this is your parish? Most people are reasonable, and they are often prepared to give us a second chance – so long as we don't push.

Sometimes *not* selling is the way to get back into selling.

Chapter 12

BE A SHOW-OFF

The rule says, don't be a bigmouth when you talk to a customer. He isn't interested in what a terrific person you are, he wants to know only one thing and that is what the product will do for him. Anything remotely resembling bragging will put him right off you and your company; he hears quite enough tall stories as it is. Try to suppress your own personality, so that when you leave he will have a clear picture of the benefits he can get from the product instead of having his ears filled with your exploits.

Makes sense, doesn't it? Nobody likes a swankpot. Yet there are occasions when we have to break this rule. This section is another reason for our keeping this book on the top shelf well out of the reach of the new boys and girls in the selling business, because if they read this and tried to apply the suggestions in it they could make the most fearful mess. What are the special occasions when we should break the rule?

I have many friends and acquaintances outside the selling game and some of them view what I do for a living with anything from amusement to the deepest suspicion. A delightful old second cousin of mine, a retired bank manager, was explaining to his wife my particular niche in the scheme of things. He said, 'Michael teaches people to *bluff* people.' She nodded in comprehension. They weren't joking; they honestly believed that salespeople needed training in deceiving, deluding and defrauding people, and that my vocation was that of a modern Fagin, teaching them to do those things more skilfully.

While most of my friends don't go as far as this in their opinion of my calling, there are those who believe that I don't really contribute anything to the pageant of life. An architect said once: 'I can't see a single instance of where I would need a salesman. I'm quite intelligent enough to know exactly what I want, whether it is a pair of shoelaces or a motor-car. The only thing a salesperson can do for me is to write out the order to my specifications, or wrap up what I buy and give me change. If they try to *sell* me anything, they get very short shrift from me.'

A fairly common reaction, especially at the level of my architect friend. The feeling, not always articulated but often in the back of people's minds, is that they know what they want and they don't need a pedlar to tell them. 'What does he know about my special circumstances, anyway.'

Faced with this attitude, and it is more prevalent than perhaps we realise, what can we do? We can suppress our personalities, fade into the background, maintain a very low profile throughout the sales call and focus instead on the product itself. Not a bad strategy and it might even work; the customer might get the feeling that the whole idea of buying was his, not ours, and with the feeling he has about salespeople, perhaps that would be the safest way to go.

The trouble is that using that format in the sales call might work well if he is buying what he has always bought, or doing what he has always done; but that is not creative selling, that is merely topping him up with the same products or services he is already using. What about if we want to change his mind? If we want him to buy a cab-over-engine truck instead of the forward-engine layout he is used to? What if we can see that what he needs is a positive-displacement compressor, not the centrifugal type which he seems so fond of? What if it is obvious that the short-term endowment policy he likes so much is ridiculous insurance for his situation and that for him, whole life, non-profit is the only way to go?

It still sounds as though we should hit the loud pedal with the product and the soft pedal with us, the salespeople, doesn't it? Then he will see the product benefits and not be put off by any defects in our personalities. In ordinary circumstances, yes, perhaps; but recognise the problem here.

[72]

This person views all of us salespeople with a sceptical eye. He doesn't think he needs us. He has a low opinion of us as contributive members of society. Therefore, anything we may say will also be viewed with suspicion, impatience and distrust, and he will simply switch off or tune out anything we may say.

And this is the time we have to stop being modest and come out of our shells. We have to show him that he can forget everything he has ever heard about or thought of the archetypal salesperson as a pedlar of gew-gaws, a low creature living on his wits who would sell his grandmother's wheelchair from under her and whose IQ is lower than his hat size.

Do you see what a delicate line we are walking here? On the one hand we have to show him that he is not dealing with a baboon, that we have the knowledge, experience and skill to help him to get what he wants and needs from the product. On the other hand – well, we could easily end up in a confrontation, and as the Chinese say, 'When you are arguing with an idiot, make sure that he is not similarly engaged.' We don't want an argument or dispute of any sort, but neither do we want the customer looking down his nose at us in contempt. This has nothing to do with our self-respect, but when he sees us as an inferior species, he is not likely to listen and accept what we say.

What we need from him, of course, is his respect. Now, respect is not something we can demand from anyone; respect has to be earned, and as salespeople we can earn it in two ways.

First, and it is something that we as salespeople tend to forget or ignore, we earn it because of the company we represent. You carry a business card with your company logo on it. Do you always realise how many doors this card opens for you which would otherwise remain shut? How many people are willing to see us, give us some of their time and listen to our sales presentation, because our company has an image of honest dealing, fair play and sound business practice over the years? I found this out very, very quickly when, after having worked all my life for highly respected companies with household names and solid reputations, I went out on my own for the first time, with only my own name and no reputation to

[73]

work for me. Don't ever sell your company's standing short; it is working for you in ways in which you may not believe. Lord, how important this can be!

I had been involved in training a group of drug salespeople as part of the launch of a new product; it was one of the cephalosporins, if you're interested. I was keen to see how it would be received in the marketplace. I happened to meet a general practitioner a few weeks later, and I asked him if he had been approached by the salesperson in his area and been given all the information about the drug. He said yes, she had told him all about it. I said, 'How does it look to you?'

He said, 'Well, the formulation seems sound, but it doesn't seem to have anything which the present cephalosporins don't have.'

'Then you won't be prescribing it?'

'Oh, yes,' he said. 'I'll give it a really good crack of the whip.'

Now I was interested. 'Why? If it doesn't seem to be any advance on anything you use now, why bother to change?'

He said, 'Because the other products I use from that company are so good that I *have* to use it and see for myself what the results are.'

Well! That is the sort of attitude in a customer that makes a salesperson think he has died and gone to heaven. Here is someone who when he is approached by a salesman immediately gives him his undivided attention and who views the presentation of the product with profound respect, and why? Because of the customer's esteem for the company.

The message here is simple: don't let us ever forget how invaluable our company's reputation, its track record and its standing in the customer's eyes can be, and how much it can help to create a climate of respect.

Sometimes we have to point out just what sort of organisation we work for. A man called on a company, asking to see someone about a type of equipment used in food-processing – he said that he might be interested in buying some of it. The divisional manager whose office the man was shown into was doubtful about the caller's credentials – after all, he had never heard of him and didn't know anything about the company who might be customers – if what this man said was true. It seemed also that the man himself was a little uneasy about the interview. The manager, half convinced that the caller was a chancer, finally said, 'I should tell you, sir, that the cheapest type of machine we are talking about costs at least £30,000.'

The caller immediately relaxed. 'Thank the Lord for that,' he said. 'To tell you the truth, I had the feeling that you people might not be able to give me the stuff we need. Now I see that you are in the big leagues, we can do business.'

As an advanced salesperson, you don't need to be warned that all this does not mean that we barge into people's offices and start shouting the odds as to just how big and successful our companies are. We know that this could easily lead to a backlash of resentment. But at the same time, let's not forget just how strong and useful a weapon the company name can be.

The second way to earn the respect of the customer is to show him that we know what we are talking about. Exactly how you go about doing this depends on your personal style, and I wouldn't try to dictate chapter and verse, to be learnt off by heart. You have to get across to him that what you say will be worth listening to, that you won't be wasting his time; at the same time, you don't want to sound like a blowhard. Compare these two statements, please:

'I have been selling plumbing supplies for sixteen years, and there's really nothing about the business that I don't know, I can promise you.'

'When I was transferred to the microfilm division, my manager wouldn't let me see a single customer until I had been through an intensive product application course at the manufacturers' training school.'

The first statement comes from the extra outsize mouth of a braggart, and it has the effect of producing two reactions from the customer; first, it irritates and offends him and second, it makes him determined to find something about the product that the salesman doesn't know. Whether or not he finds this, the sales call has degenerated into a contest instead of a presentation, and any real chance of a sale has been lost.

The second statement says, in a way which surely can't

[75]

offend, 'You are not dealing with a clown. My company wouldn't send someone out to waste the time of busy people like you. We can talk at the same level.'

This is not swanking. Here you are showing your credentials, giving the customer a reason to listen to you. Think about it: doesn't he have a right to know that the recommendations, advice and suggestions you are giving him are based on solid knowledge and experience, rather than on thirty minutes of leafing through a product catalogue? Glance at the following examples and I believe that you will agree that, introduced at the right time, they will help to create customer confidence in you and a respect for your opinions and counsel.

'We have a monthly forum where we salespeople sit down with our engineers to discuss the technical side of our products. It's amazing how much we learn there which can help customers like you to get more out of your factory.'

'From being involved in selling to your industry, I think that I can handle most problems that occur. However, one thing my experience has taught me is that there is a time to call in the technician, and I won't hesitate to do that if I find anything in your operation which needs his specialised help.'

'Theoretical knowledge is all very well, but I also spent six months doing the merchandising for the Diamond chain of department stores, and you know how high their standards have always been.'

Don't ever be shy or falsely modest about showing the customer that you know what you are talking about. If you do it the right way, it won't offend him; on the contrary, it will help to instil in him the confidence and respect which you need before you start selling.

Chapter 13

TELL HIM THAT YOUR PRICE IS TOO HIGH

The rule says, when the customer complains about your high price you don't argue with him. One of the first things we learnt was the old saw, 'Win an argument and lose a sale.' All right, as advanced salespeople we can agree with that.

However, the rule goes on to say something like this: while we don't argue with the customer, neither do we agree with him when he says that the price is too high.

Well, if we are not allowed to agree with him then we have no alternative but to disagree with him, not so? Disagreeing is pretty close to arguing, and the trouble is that the salesperson can find himself in a position where, without realising it and certainly without wanting it, he is insisting that the price isn't too high and the customer is equally adamant that the price is too high. Now, if that isn't an argument, it will do until one comes along.

Don't agree with the customer when he says your price is too high. On the other hand, don't whatever you do, argue with him. Whichever we choose, we could be in trouble, so let's break the rule and when he says, 'Your price is too high!', let's agree with him and see what happens.

While ten thousand sales trainers go into shock at this suggestion that we disregard one of their most sacred tenets, let us see what would happen in a sales call if we said, 'You are absolutely right, sir; the price *is* too high.' Well, the first thing that would happen is that all the wind would be taken out of the customer's sails. It would be the very last thing that he expected to hear from us. Not that we want the listener to feel awkward or embarrassed; we merely want him to continue to listen to us. He has been told a price and his reaction has been, 'That's too much.' He has then *closed his mind*. He has no desire to continue the conversation, he has lost interest. You almost certainly don't have the authority to drop the price, and he doesn't expect you to haggle about it. 'That's too high,' he says. End of story.

So, to his astonishment, the salesperson readily agrees with him. 'Right!' he says. 'The price *is* too high.' What happens? What happens is that his mind, which has snapped shut, swings open again. This does not mean that he has changed his mind about the price; quite the contrary, in fact, since the person who is supposed to be selling the product apparently agrees with him that what he is selling is overpriced. What it does mean is that he is prepared to continue the conversation. You have made him curious, you see, and curiosity is, as you well know, one of the strongest compulsions in the world.

There is another aspect to this, and it is one which I have mentioned over and over again when discussing the price problem in a training clinic. When a customer fixes his beady eye on you and tells you that your price is too high, he is not merely telling, he is *watching*. He wants to see your reaction to the price objection, and he confidently expects that you will shatter into a million bits before his eyes. He believes that you are dreading hearing anything to do with the price and that he will see fear, confusion and abject surrender in your expression.

So, instead, what does he see? He sees you nodding in apparent agreement. Not only that, but he sees no signs of worry or fright on your countenance; you seem to be in complete command of your emotions and totally at ease. Believe me, that conversation has just been re-opened. But where do you go from there? You have managed to keep the conversation going, but perhaps you have managed to swim away from the *Titanic* only to be picked up by the *Lusitania*; you are in no better situation than you were before. Here is an example of what could happen, and it is the justification for telling the customer that yes, the price is indeed too high. The product is an electric razor and the time is some years in the past when the brilliant invention of rechargeable appliances was very new; few people had even heard of the idea and fewer still had any experience of them. The prices were of course much, much higher than the conventional products and sales executives knew that there would be strong resistance to the price from the retailers, who would fear that their customers would have a certain price range in their minds for an electric razor and would never consider raising their sights enough to buy the rechargeable model. It would therefore be necessary to face the problem head-on when selling-in to the retailers; it was felt that no conventional approach would work.

'Sorry, but no sale. It looks like a quality product, all right, but there is no way that any of my usual customers will ever pay that for a razor; the price is way out of line. I'm sorry we can't do business, and thanks for coming in.'

'You believe that the retail price is too high?'

'I don't just *believe* it's too high, I *know* it is. I have sold in this area for nearly seventeen years, and I know the market. Too high. Now, if you'll excuse me – '

'I agree with you, sir. It *is* too high.'

'What did you say?'

'I said you were right; the price is too high.'

'Do you mean to tell me that you came in here to sell me a product knowing that the price is over the top? With that attitude, how many of those things have you sold, anyway? And what would your sales manager say if he knew you were going around telling people that it is overpriced?'

'Oh, he agrees with me. You see, what we are asking for this razor is completely unrealistic – if all that people want is an electric razor.'

'Well, that *is* all that people want. And what is that thing *but* an electric razor, anyway? It's electric, it shaves off the bristles, that's it, right?'

'Right – a wonderful product, but priced too high for just a razor.'

'You keep saying that. How do you expect to sell it, and what's more, how do you expect *me* to sell it if, as you admit, it's overpriced?'

'You know, sir, you asked how many of these we have sold. At our weekly sales meeting yesterday, my sales director told us that so far the launch has exceeded the forecast by more than twenty-five per cent. Now, would all those stores have bought it unless they thought they could sell it?'

'That's their business; this is mine, and the people who walk into this shop won't pay that for a razor.'

'Your decision, of course. You get a middle-class clientele here, I imagine; quite a lot of businessmen. Most of them do a bit of travelling in their work.'

'Sure, that's why they buy electric razors.'

'Correct. But what a nuisance it is to find that the plug on your razor doesn't fit the socket in the hotel room – or even that there isn't a socket at all! This razor is rechargeable, and that means the businessman simply takes it off the charging stand at home, slips it into his bag, and it is fully charged with a guarantee of five shaves before it needs to be charged again. What a convenience!'

'No wires, flex or anything like that? No plugging in?'

'None, and think what a safety factor you have here. Most electric razors are used in bathrooms, and that means wet floors and water in baths and basins – drop an ordinary electric razor into water and you have a killer appliance. Drop this one in and you pick it out and wipe it off.'

'Uh huh.'

'Convenience and safety. Now, the shaving action itself. Lower-priced razors have a rather thick shaving foil – the strip of metal covering the cutting blades – and it really isn't possible to get a shave as smooth as a blade razor. This one has a shaving foil as thin as a quarter of a human hair – if you shave once with it you will feel as though a barber has just done his stuff with brush, lather and a cut-throat; the closeness of the shave is almost unbelievable.'

'That so? A really close shave?'

'Close? My father-in-law has had to shave twice a day all his life; he has a very heavy growth. I gave him one of these for Father's Day and since then he can get away with one shave a day. So; convenience, safety, and the closest shave possible. Now, let's look at the next . . . '

At first glance that sales talk seems to have little in it which you haven't seen before and probably done yourself, many times. The salesman is merely piling one benefit on top of the

that is to keep talking. A good listener is far more rare than an adequate lover.   *Nightmare in Pink*, 1964

That seems to wrap it up, and in almost all cases it does. Here we are talking about the very special situation where simply ignoring the customer's remarks can be the only way to keep the sales talk going and make the sale. We are about to look at a few examples of this, but unless you are an advanced salesperson, please stop reading and come back in ten years' time; this is not for you.

The scene is the office of the stationery buyer of a chain of department stores. Present is the buyer, the brand manager of a company selling paper and allied products, and me. The manager has told me that without fail he is going to sell his Christmas Wrapping package to this prospect. The package consists of an attractive display of gift-wrapping paper, tags, ribbons and tapes. So far this buyer has turned the special offer down flat, three years running. The manager is convinced that the package is an absolute natural for this chain of stores; his experience tells him that it will sell up a storm if it is only given a chance.

Buyer: No. Not the Christmas package. I like your products and you know that I'm a regular punter of yours, but not the Christmas package.
Manager (*in an easy, relaxed manner*):   It's a real eye-catcher this year, isn't it? I didn't think that our design people could improve on last year's designs – and that one sold like wildfire – but they have made this year's even better.
Buyer: Yes, but as I've told you every year, this sort of thing is not for us.
Manager: What makes it such an attractive deal is the extra ten per cent discount for twenty or more, and of course with your thirty-two outlets you immediately qualify.
Buyer: But don't you understand? This is not the sort of line we stock.
Manager: Incredible how the design people have been able to put so much product into such a compact space – it fits easily on to the counter near the till, and your customers can't

resist taking a few items from it. Last year it was the fastest-moving product we had ever produced.

Buyer: You don't seem to be listening to me; *we do not sell this type of product.*

Manager: Last year we made a quick survey and we found that stores which stocked the display increased their unit sales at that counter by thirteen per cent – remarkable, isn't it?

Buyer (*looking helplessly at me*): *Tell* this maniac that this line is not for us! (*I shrug my shoulders; if he won't listen to the customer, he certainly won't listen to me.*)

Manager: You'll find when the packages are placed in your stores that the items which run out first are the ribbons and tags. We recommend that you take an extra case of each so that you can replace as the packages empty – you don't want bare spots on the displays, do you?

Buyer: No. (*Realising what he has said*) But that doesn't apply to us anyway.

Manager: Of course, what makes the deal irresistible is that even after the Christmas rush, you can dismantle the display and put most of the items into your non-seasonal stock. Have you ever had Christmas or Easter or Mothering Day items over with no chance of selling them?

Buyer: Yes, sometimes.

Manager: That's why you are going to like this package; there's no risk of that. High profit, compact size, increase of unit sales by thirteen per cent, mostly year-round, non-seasonal items. Can you honestly say that you can afford to turn your back on this fantastic bargain?

Buyer (*sarcastically*): Don't tell me that you are actually asking for my opinion? You haven't listened to a word I've said so far.

Manager: Goodness me, of course I need your opinion! After all, whether or not you buy is your decision.

Buyer: I'm delighted to hear it.

Manager: Do you agree that your eight biggest outlets should have two displays each? Makes sense. That means a nice round number of forty displays altogether.

Buyer: Does it indeed.

Manager: As I said, there's an extra ten per cent for twenty or more. Since you are taking twice that number I think we can go for another two and a half per cent. This is something we haven't done for any other customer, but of course, you are a special case.

Buyer: Oh, for God's sake, where do I sign? I warn you, if this line doesn't sell, I'll have your guts for garters.

Manager: If it doesn't sell, I'll cut them out myself. Thank you.

You are probably shaking your head and saying to yourself, 'Nonsense; you can't sell that way. That scenario was a figment of imagination.' Not at all, it actually happened, and as near as I can remember it, almost word for word. Now, why did it work when it flouted one of the major rules of person-to-person selling, which states that when the customer talks, we listen? Well, the circumstances were favourable. First, that customer, while he had never bought the Christmas package before, was a long-term customer of the company and had faith in its products. Second, the brand manager had known the buyer some time and had the buyer's confidence as being someone who knew his products and his market. This allowed him to talk in a way in which he probably would not have done to a relative stranger. He realised that, in this case, sticking to the rule would get him nowhere; he had tried it that way in previous years and it hadn't worked. The only way to get all the advantages of the product across to the customer was simply not to listen to him when he said 'No'.

You might like to try this when you have been turned down flat by someone who you are absolutely certain will benefit by having your product. Your attitude should be relaxed, laid-back and, in this case especially, non-aggressive. Your tone of voice and manner are quietly confident that he will buy when he has all the facts, and you are in the process of giving him those facts. It works; in an astonishing number of cases, it really does work.

There is another situation where not listening to the customer can work better than anything else. This will remind you of the chapter where we looked at a situation where we should actually laugh at the customer. Perhaps if the idea of laughing in his face appalled you, then here is another way which could

[85]

work just as well. The situation is the same; he has said something which is absolutely untrue and you have to squash it right away before it gets out and ruins everything. Why do people do this sort of thing? To put you off your stride, to take the mickey, or plain, simple bloody-mindedness? Whatever the reason, the worst thing we can do is rise to the bait, because that is exactly what the customer wants you to do. In the following example, our salesman has leapt at the fly like a short-sighted trout, with horrific results:

' – And the whole unit is guaranteed for three years, which is unusually good for this type of product – '

'Yes, except that when your company goes bankrupt as I hear it is going to do, the guarantee won't be worth very much, will it?'

'Bankrupt? My company isn't going bankrupt!'

'Well, maybe not, but no smoke without fire, as they say. Otherwise where did the story come from? Must be something in it.'

'There's nothing in it! I would have heard if it was true!'

'Now, don't get so upset. I think you'd better go back and ask your directors whether you'll still have a job in three *months*, never mind the three years of your guarantee.'

Clear victory for the heckler and defeat for the salesperson. Whatever happens now, the sale is certainly lost. Apart from everything else, the listener has got himself so involved with the rumour that he probably believes it himself, whether or not he did when he first voiced it. Worse than that, he even seems to have succeeded in putting a seed of doubt in the salesman's mind.

Well, we can handle this sort of thing, where the customer says something which is either patently untrue or insulting or both, by laughing at it, as we have seen earlier. It may be that the situation is one where laughter would be an unnatural reaction on our part, and personal insults would fit into that category. In this case the very best way to handle it is simply not to listen to it. By ignoring it, you can show the customer that it is really not worth discussing, whereas if we answer the charge we can immediately give him the edge in the verbal duel.

[86]

It *is* a duel, of course. Do we need to discuss this? In an earlier chapter I tried to make the point that we are not engaged in a friendly conversation with the customer. We may *be* on friendly terms with him of course, and it may be better for our chances if we are, but a friendly conversation is something which you and I have over a glass in the corner pub. If I am trying to get you to do something which you see no reason to do, then that is a duel. The difference between that duel and those of yore when two men met at dawn and only one walked away from the meeting is that in our duel there is no loser; there are two winners. In the true creative sale both the customer and the salesperson win, and as an advanced salesperson you don't need me to explain to you why this is so.

Back to the situation where he has said something which is so clearly untrue that answering it would only tend to give it credence and worth. He says it and we ignore it. Perhaps that is enough and he drops it, but perhaps this is one of those persistent characters and he repeats it, watching closely for your reaction. The very best thing to do now, and you will have to try this yourself to understand how effective it is, is to look at him and let a slow, confident smile develop on your face. It is a smile which says, 'Come on, now; you and I are too intelligent to believe that.' I have seen many people smile back, a trifle sheepishly, and drop the subject, without the salesperson having to say a single word – in fact, ignoring the remark or allegation entirely.

What we are discussing here are the subtleties of inter-personal relationships, of course, which is a rather pompous term for how people get on with each other. I have a horror of sounding mystical or too profound about this subject, but I believe that what the customer does in this sort of situation stems from the fact that, in the sales call, the salesperson is usually in the office, factory, shop or home of the customer – on the customer's turf, in fact. Thus he is almost a guest of the customer, yet who is doing most of the talking? Who is running the interview? Why, the salesperson! Therefore we as salespeople are in charge in a place where, usually, the customer is in charge – at least, this is the way that customers

[87]

could very well feel. So it is natural for them to want to get into the act and to assert their authority, and one way to do this is to put us off our stroke by saying something calculated to irritate, worry or depress us. Let us show for one instant that they have got to us and we have lost; show that what they have said doesn't bother us and we have won in a bloodless battle which has done no one any harm.

Listen to the customer? An essential rule, ninety-nine times out of a hundred. The hundredth time, ignore the customer and go on to a successful sale.

Chapter 15

KNOCK THE COMPETITION

Well, the writer of this work has finally gone completely mad. You have been able to live with most of the suggestions so far, but there is no way that you can ever agree with this one. Not knocking the competitive product, company or salespeople has from time immemorial been one of the pillars of wisdom of selling. It was one of the very first things you were taught when you entered the business. It was emphasised that there were no exceptions to this rule. You may even have been told by your first sales manager that if he ever caught you running down the opposition he would exact the most terrible vengeance.

Defaming, denigrating, vilifying and generally running down the enemy in selling is such a universally abhorred practice that it hardly seems necessary to give the reasons for not doing it, but it may be worthwhile to iterate why knocking is not on and why the no-knocking rule is such a good one:

• It is unethical
In every field of endeavour there are laws of good manners and good taste, from politics to sport, from social life to business, and maligning your competitor transgresses the most fundamental of these.

• It invites reprisals
Man is a weird animal; when you attack him, he fights back. Make a practice of knocking and you will be truly knocked in return.

• It shows fear of the opposition

In most cases, it is the better product which is attacked in this way, not the worse one. When a salesperson spends most of the time beating on his opposition, it shows that the product is a good one and therefore to be feared. Nobody bothers even to mention a product which is no threat to them.

• It focuses attention on the opposition

One of the silliest results to come from attacking the enemy is that the customer, who may until then not even have thought of any other product, now sees a spotlight beamed away from our product and at another product, and who has provided the light for the beam? We have. Great! We have given time to the opposition on a programme that we have paid for.

• It indicates mediocre selling ability

This is the most important reason of all to avoid knocking. If the only way you can sell me your product is to tell me how awful the other product is, then you brand yourself as a second-rate salesperson. 'Well, perhaps we aren't as good as all that, but at least we are better than those other characters,' is a pretty sleazy way to sell, and the image we project when we sell like this is that of a third-rate salesperson flogging fourth-rate products.

That should be enough, don't you think? Five good, sound reasons not to say one word which could be construed as running down the opposition. 'Don't knock' has to be one of the strongest commandments in good salesmanship, a rule which should never under any conceivable circumstances be broken.

So let us examine some situations where the advanced salesperson could break the rule.

The scene is a large public library, and the salesperson is talking to the librarian who is in charge of repairing books which have been damaged in some way – pages torn, spines broken.

'No, thank you. I don't need your gums and tapes. When I took over this job last month I called in a representative of the

Quikstik Company, and she recommended a tape and a glue for fixing the books. So there really is no point in buying from two suppliers, is there?'

'Not if you're completely satisfied. How are the products working?'

'Well, I haven't started using them yet. They were delivered only last week and I'm still getting organised. I'm sure they will be all right, though. The salesman assured me that they were two of their fastest-selling lines.'

'That's fine. Do you mind if I ask what the products are? Just for my own interest.'

'I don't remember the names, but the cartons are next door. Come and see.'

'Oh, dear.'

'What do you mean, "Oh, dear"? Don't tell me that there is anything wrong with these products.'

'I have to tell you that there is everything wrong with these products, and that if you use them on your books, you will have a disaster on your hands.'

'That's enough. You are only saying that because I bought from another company instead of from you. Do you think that's an ethical way to do business?'

'Ethical or not, ma'am, what you are hearing is the truth. If you use that stuff on your books, you will regret it.'

'But the other representative told me that this glue is the strongest available!'

'It is. But what she apparently didn't tell you was that it dries into a hard, inflexible substance. Now, if you use it to repair the spine of a book, the first time you try to open the book you will either break the spine or tear out a page.'

'I don't believe you!'

'Believe me. I know that product, and while it may be all right for other applications, it should never have been recommended when a flexible join is needed.'

'But why should they sell me a product which doesn't work? I suppose you have something nasty to say about the tape as well?'

'Yes, I do. That tape will look fine on the books for about four months, then it will begin to discolour and pull away from the page.'

[91]

'Why?'

'Because it is a viscose-based tape, which means that it is made from wood-pulp, and that means that it is bio-degradable. Now that's fine for anti-pollution, but it is absolutely useless for permanent repair of paper. Don't put it into a single book; if you do you'll regret it.'

'I suppose you have a tape which won't do the things you say this one will do.'

'Yes, we do. It's a polyester-based tape with a permanent adhesive and it will last as long as the book does.'

'I still find this difficult to believe. Why should that other representative recommend – what did you call it – viscose tape?'

'Probably because her company doesn't have polyester tapes in their range.'

'And the glue? You said it sets hard. Naturally, you have one which stays soft?'

'You bet. Permanent flexing of the bond; no matter how many times you bend it, you'll never break the join or tear the pages.'

'Doesn't the other company have one of those glues? Perhaps I could change this for the correct product.'

'Perhaps you could, but why should you deal with a crowd that has already sold you two products which won't work and that would have put you into real trouble if you had used them? I have stopped you from making a big mistake. Which company do you think deserves your business?'

'So you are telling me to send this stuff back and buy your glue and tape instead?'

'I couldn't have put it better myself, ma'am.'

What do you think of that example? I imagine you don't like it very much. You are probably saying something like, 'All right, so he had to point out why the two products were not the right choice, but he could have done it by extolling the virtues of the right products instead of running down – knocking, in fact – the wrong ones.'

Maybe, but the librarian gave him a flat turn-down right at the start of the interview. She was perfectly happy with the products she had bought and totally confident that they would do a fine job for her. It was necessary to shake her out of her complacent attitude and the only way to do this was to hit the opposition very hard indeed. No hinting or suggesting or recommending would do in this situation; that customer had to be told in very direct terms that the opposition products were wrong, that the opposition salesperson had ripped her off – there is really no other term for it. The salesperson must have known what her products would do, and at worst she had deliberately lied to her. Even at best, she had been woefully lacking in knowledge of her products.

This last point is what would bother most people about that example. In a hard-sell situation, it is considered acceptable to say that your product is better than the opposition but you don't ever, under any circumstances, say a word against the salesperson. Yet here the salesman has come right out and said in so many words that the enemy was guilty of lying, misrepresenting, or knowing so little about her own products that she wasn't fit to hold her job. That is certainly breaking the rule, and how can we possibly justify it?

When we tread on ice as thin as this we have to realise one thing: that if we are wrong in one tiny aspect – if we are unable to back up one single word of our claims – we are history. We will be shown the door and it is doubtful we would ever be able to call on that customer again, much less sell her anything. What makes the ground so dangerous to tread, and this applies to that last example, is that when we knock the opposition product we are also insulting the customer. We are saying loud and clear, 'Not only is this a bad product, but you must have been very stupid to have bought it in the first place.' This is hardly what we could call good customer relations. Worse – not only will the customer resent this implication but she will tend to leap to the defence of the product which she has bought, and this is the *real* danger of knocking. I have bought a tennis racket or a microwave oven and it has turned out to be less than satisfactory. I can complain loudly and bitterly that I was sold a pup and I probably shall, but don't *you* come along and tell me that my purchase is a lemon or I shall deny the charge and probably resent you for making it.

So, knock the opposition and the customer's reaction could be, 'I don't care if your product *is* so marvellous, I'm sticking to this one, and you get out of here.'

All very good reasons for not knocking, and strong warnings against the practice *unless it is unavoidable* – and sometimes it is.

In the last example the claim was against the company's products and, by implication, the salesperson of the company. In this next one the company itself is under the spotlight.

A small company has submitted a low quotation for tractors which will be digging trenches and laying over six hundred miles of oil pipe. The tender stipulates that the supplier will have to set up service depots along the pipeline and provide technicians at these depots; also that they will have a full supply of parts and equipment for the tractors. Don Leeds, sales engineer for a larger company than the one which submitted the low tender, is talking to the chief buyer of the construction company which called for the tender and which will be laying the pipeline.

Buyer: It's no good giving me your sales talk, Leeds. I know your products probably as well as you do, and I know how good they are. The fact remains that this new crowd has put in a very keen price and I don't think you can come anywhere near it.

Leeds: Quite right, Mr Sutton. We can't.

Buyer: And please don't try to tell me that your tractors are marvellous and these are junk. I have been quite deeply into their specifications and they are really quite impressive. Perhaps not quite as good as yours, but it's a very good-looking machine.

Leeds: I agree. As you say, perhaps not quite up to the standard of ours, but certainly a sound design, and the specs seem to be good.

Buyer: Well! It's nice to hear a salesman admit that his opposition has a good product. So, since you say that the tractor is good, and I say that the price fits beautifully into my budget, why are you here?

Leeds: I'm here to advise you not to accept their quote.

Buyer: That is an extraordinary statement. I suppose you will now advise me to buy yours instead.

Leeds: I'd like you to take mine, obviously, but if not mine then one of the other big companies; anything except that particular quote.

Buyer: Would you like to explain yourself? And I should warn you that you are close to being asked to leave and not come back here.

Leeds: Mr Sutton, that company's product is quite acceptable, as we both recognise. I know the salesman who called on you – Ted York. I should know him; he worked for us before he moved over to this new bunch. He's a good man and he knows the earth-moving business back to front. Ted would do a good job for you and so would his tractors – what would let you down if you accepted that quote would be the company itself. As you know, they started up only four months ago when they got the franchise for the K W K tractor and equipment. Mr Sutton, they simply won't live up to the terms of the tender.

Buyer: They'll have to. The contract they will sign will tie them down so tightly there is no way they will be able to wriggle out of any part of it.

Leeds: That may be, but I promise you they won't be able to honour it.

Buyer: Now listen here, Leeds. You are making some very wild statements about another company. What have you got to back up what you say? Talk fast or get out of here and don't come back.

Leeds: I don't blame you for feeling like that, Mr Sutton. It's not nice for a salesman to shout the odds about another company, and it's not something I usually do. But in this case I know I'm right. That company can't comply with the commitments it has made in that quote. I don't have to read their tender to know what the commitments are; they are the same ones we made in our quote.

Buyer: Give me one concrete example of what you mean.

Leeds: I'll give you two. First, parts availability. You require a 90 per cent on-the-spot availability of all wearing parts and 100 per cent in seven days; they can't do it. As you know, their product comes from the Far East, and it's common knowledge that they are having trouble getting parts for the machines they have imported already, never mind any new ones.

Buyer: Is that true, or is that just a rumour you people have thought up?

Leeds: I can give you the names of three companies who have tractors standing idle waiting for parts. Everything I'm saying can be checked, Mr Sutton; I'd be an idiot to lie to you about this. Next, technical staff. They hired one of our technical people away from us and he came back to his old job last week. He says that they are stretched to their limit on technicians, with people already working sixteen to twenty hours' overtime a week. Ask yourself if you can afford to put yourself into a situation where you would have to rely on a company like that.

Buyer: Well, if all that is true then it could – *could*, mind you – change my thinking. You are saying that this company has over-extended itself just to get the order?

Leeds: That's just about the size of it.

Buyer: But why would they do that if they know that they won't be able to comply with the conditions of the agreement? Do they think that once the work has started, we'll be committed to them and unable to change to another supplier, so we will waive some of the conditions?

Leeds: I've no idea.

Buyer: Well, I'll have to talk to my directors about this.

Leeds: Do you want me to take any action at all?

Buyer: No thanks, you've ruined my day enough as it is. I thought I had this all tied up and you come in with this stuff. You may hear from me later in the week. I warn you, I'm going to be doing some checking, and unless what you say stands up, you are in trouble.

And how do you like that as an example of bad-mouthing the opposition? Don Leeds couldn't have gone much further down that road than he did. At first sight, it would seem that there could be no justification for what he said; here, it would seem, is your typical high-pressure artist, going for the sale no matter what it takes, and if it means slandering the opposition, then so be it.

Possibly, but if you examine exactly what he said, you realise that while it was a damning indictment, at no stage did Leeds voice an *opinion* of the other company. He hit very hard indeed, but he produced only facts, and they were facts that could be checked. Also, he managed to get across to the buyer that the reason for his call was not merely the sour grapes attitude of someone who has lost a sale against tough competition and is therefore venting his ill temper and bile; he really did seem to be concerned at the problems the buyer's company would face if they committed themselves to using the smaller company's plant.

Finally, and it was the best thing Leeds did, he resisted the temptation offered by the buyer to impute unethical motives to the other company. The buyer asked him if he thought that the smaller company reckoned on getting away with it, once the agreement was signed, because of the difficulty the buyer would have in changing to another supplier once the job was under way. Leeds managed to avoid this trap; he merely said, 'I've no idea.'

Knocking? Yes, he knocked the opposition, but there was no other way to get his message across. The truth was that the smaller company was not being completely ethical in tendering on something they must have known they couldn't live up to and they invited the sort of treatment they got.

One more example? A dyestuffs manufacturer made a breakthrough with a new type of yellow dye. Apparently, yellow is a tricky colour in the dyestuffs industry because it tends to fade more than other colours in direct sunlight. Well, this company produced a yellow dye which resisted fading to a much greater extent than other yellow dyes. The following scene was soon being enacted in the factories of many textile manufacturers:

'Yes, I know who you are; you've called on me before. I told you then and I tell you now, I'm satisfied with my present supplier of dyes. No reason to change, unless you have suddenly chopped your prices?'

'No. Our prices are competitive, sir; we can't cut them.'

'By "competitive", I suppose you mean that they are about the same as I'm paying now? As I say, no reason to change.'

[97]

'Tell me: have you ever had come-backs on textiles which you have dyed yellow, and the complaint is that they have faded badly in strong sunlight?'

'Well, sure; we get the occasional problem. But yellow is always affected by direct sunlight.'

'Not *our* yellow.'

'What?'

'I said, not *our* yellow.'

'You're trying to tell me that you have a yellow that won't fade as badly as other yellows?'

'That's exactly what I'm saying, sir.'

'Now, wait a minute. It sounds as though you are saying that the opposition is making an inferior product.'

'Compared with ours, and as far as fading goes, yes.'

'That's a very arrogant attitude. What gives you the right to run down the other manufacturers like that?'

'This does.' (She produces the results of an independent test of four different yellow dyes which were exposed to ultra-violet light for 100 hours.) 'Sample A is ours and B, C and D are our chief opposition. C is the dye you are using now. As you can see, when I say ours is the best, I'm not talking hot air.'

'Who did this test, your younger brother?'

'Worthington Laboratories, and my brother doesn't work for them. Why not telephone them and check? Mr Teale is the man who was in charge of the tests.'

'No. Look, if the yellow really is colour-fast, then perhaps I'll take a few gallons. What's your minimum quantity?'

'*Minimum* quantity? And only the yellow? Don't you think that if one of our dyes is as good as all that, you should seriously consider standardising on the whole colour range? You can qualify for the bulk discount if you take twenty gallons of any one colour, and another five per cent if you – '

We can leave this salesperson now, getting stuck into her sales proposal and, it would seem, holding quite a strong hand. Let us examine her presentation. She came out flat-footed and said that the opposition product was inferior, and by definition, that is knocking. Was it really necessary to do that? Wouldn't it have been just as effective if she had talked

[98]

positively about her product instead of negatively about the other product? This is really what it all boils down to, isn't it? It is much nicer to say, 'Ours is good,' rather than, 'Theirs is bad.' More pleasant, more ethical, and with no danger that we will be labelled high-pressure artists or similar low characters.

Nicer to do it that way, perhaps, but sometimes it simply doesn't work. When someone is strongly tied to a certain way of doing something by habit, tradition, temperament or simply ignorance of a better way of doing it, it often is not enough to say, 'See how good we are!' In that situation, showing the benefits he could enjoy may not be strong enough to jerk him out of the deep groove he is occupying. We have to show him the losses he is incurring by using another product, and if that entails showing him that the product is actually inferior to ours, or that the company lacks facilities that ours has, or that their people do not have the experience of our people, then that is what we have to do.

We have spent some time on this section, because at first sight the idea of running down the opposition seems completely unacceptable. Not only is it apparently wrong from a moral point of view; almost worse than that, it seems to be pragmatically unsound and even counter-productive. Yet there are times when it has to be done, and it *can* be done so long as we recognise two important qualifications:

First, we should be absolutely sure of our facts. Second, we should stick to facts and avoid giving opinions. 'Their product will never last as long as ours, and here's why' is acceptable. 'That's a sleazy product' is not.

Don't ever knock competition? Why not? Break the rule and make the sale.

Chapter 16

DON'T BOTHER ABOUT SALES
VOLUME

One of the great truths which was revealed to us early in our selling careers – perhaps even on the first day we reported for duty – was the fact that we had been hired first, last and always to Move Product.

'On your new business card it says *sales*man or -woman,' we were told. 'And that means exactly what it says. Your value to the company is in direct proportion to the sales you bring in every day. And don't forget,' our sales manager went on, 'when I talk about sales I mean *actual* sales. I mean sales where you have the customer all nicely tied up with his signature on the dotted line. I don't mean sales which might happen next month or next year, I mean sales *today*. I can't live on promises, I'm not interested in the future. I'm interested in right *now*.'

So we became today people rather than tomorrow people, interested in the sales which we had in our order books this afternoon and which we had written this morning. If we had read Omar Khayyám, we would have agreed with the poet when he talked about 'Unborn tomorrow and dead yesterday'. Only today's sales meant anything at all.

It's a good rule, because it forces us to keep our heads out of the air, dreaming about those big orders which *might* just happen in the future. For new salespeople it instils a sense of immediacy about their job; it makes them realise that they are only as good as their last sale.

A good rule, but we as advanced salespeople must break it if we are to progress into the big time in selling.

To investigate just how and when to break this rule let us go back to an aspect of that unexciting and uninspiring part of our early training known as Time And Territory Planning. Throw your mind back to the section known as Call Frequency, where we were shown how to grade customers so as to decide how often to call on them. Gradings vary with different industries and from company to company, but a typical grading chart could look something like this:

Grade	Yearly sales volume	Calls per year
A	Over £50,000	24
B	£40 to £50,000	18
C	£30 to £40,000	12
D	£15 to £30,000	6
E	Under £15,000	3

Don't worry if those figures are nowhere near those of your industry; toothpaste companies have very different sales volumes and gradings from tankship companies. It is the concept we are looking at here, and any set of figures will do to illustrate our point. Now as we can see, we were taught to call more frequently on the bigger spenders and less frequently on the smaller fry. This, we were told, was to ensure that we used our time to the best advantage; after all, the high-volume buyers were the ones who paid our salaries with their big orders, so it made sense to call on them frequently and generally to stay as close to them as dew on a rose petal.

All well and good, but how long was it before one of those big buyers nailed us with a hard eye and said something like this: 'Here again? Perhaps you had better punch a time card along with the other employees. Look, mate, you seem to be turning up here about twice a month, and frankly, that's too often. Your product is doing a good job for me, I'm happy with your company's service, and I re-order every six weeks. If anything should go wrong, I have your business and your home phone numbers in my book. Now, why don't you cut your calls by half, or even a quarter, and save yourself and me some time?'

It has happened, hasn't it? Yes, it has, and more than once. But your sales manager seemed to be in love with the grading system as a way of calculating call frequency, so you simply changed that grade A customer to a grade B *for the purpose of calling*, and no blood was shed.

Then you noticed an interesting thing with one of your D grade customers. You saw that they had bought five acres of ground behind their factory and were clearing the land. Also, the buyer asked you if it would be possible for him to order products from you which could be delivered in other centres. You realised that what was happening here was a big expansion of the company, although at the moment they were still buying at the D rate – between £15,000 and £30,000. What did you do? You immediately promoted them to the B grade *for the purpose of calling*, ignoring the present buying level.

So, in the first example, we ignored the sales volume because of special circumstances and at the express request of the customer. In the second, we ignored sales volume – present sales volume, that is – and focused instead on possible future sales. I included the first example merely to stress that we always need to be flexible when looking at call frequency, but it is the second example which is really interesting. Here we are ignoring present sales and concentrating on future potential, and it is the *potential* which should command all our attention.

Forget sales volume; work on sales *potential*.

There is a salesman somewhere who is still alive, only because I didn't happen to have a gun on me at the right time; if I had been armed I would have shot him dead. I had taken over a team of industrial oil salesmen, and I was going out with each of them in turn to get a feeling of what was happening out there. This day we were in his car and I had his customer file on my lap, looking through the cards. I said, 'According to this you have a customer along here somewhere.'

He said, 'That's right, he's just ahead.' I saw that the customer bought small; a few gallons of low-grade automotive oil every now and then. I wondered what his potential might be, until we got out of the car and walked into the customer's place of business, and it was then that I felt like committing murder.

The customer was a lawnmower repair shop, a one-man business on the edge of town. He ordered five gallons of oil from us and offered us a cup of tea. My salesman looked as though he would have enjoyed a cuppa, but a look at my face gave him the idea it was not tea-time.

When we were back in the car I took several slow, deep breaths and said, 'I hope you made the most of that call because it is the last time you will ever call on that man. In fact, from today, he is no longer a customer of yours.'

He was astounded. 'But he has just given me an order! It was a successful sales call!'

I said, 'It was a disaster of a sales call. In the first place, we will have travelled a total of eight miles out of our way in order to make the call. In the process, we used up forty-five minutes out of your selling day. The profit we shall make on five gallons of monograde won't even begin to pay for the mileage, not to speak of the time. Damn it, he should never have been a customer of ours; he should be buying that oil from the service station around the corner. Just the cost of keeping him on our books means that each order is a dead loss. You can phone him and tell him why you won't be calling again and why he is being taken off the customer list.'

My salesman drove for a while with a sulky look on his face. Suddenly he brightened; he had caught me out in an inconsistency. He said, 'You were perfectly happy this morning when we went just as far out of our way to call on that canning company, and all they buy from us is a few pounds of grease for their electric motors. Why, their order wasn't even as much in value as the lawnmower chap's!'

I did some more slow breathing. 'I was delighted to make the call on the canning company with you, because they use a lot of oil products. At the moment they buy only the lithium grease from us, but you can see that they like the product and it won't be long before you get in with our oils, and later, when the present contract expires, with the fuels – petrol and diesel.'

'But that's for the future,' he objected.

'Exactly. As far as you are concerned, the canning company

has a future and the lawnmower shop hasn't. He will never be a big enough customer to justify calling on him. Even if he goes mad and doubles his business and opens two more branches, he will still be a dead loss to us.'

It took more than that one chat to convince him that present sales volume is important for today, certainly, and we don't dare neglect it; but for a growth territory as part of a growth company, what is all-important is the potential of the customer.

When setting out your call cycle and determining call frequency, don't bother with sales *volume* – look for sales *potential*.

Chapter 17

SELL THE *BAD* NEWS

When I was selling life insurance my manager had one article of faith which he never got tired of airing. Again and again at sales meetings, he would say, 'You are selling *life* insurance, not *death* insurance. You bring good news to the customer, not bad news. I don't want any of you characters to sell negatively. People don't like hearing negative things, they want to hear positive things. Remember that, will you? Always sell positively!'

Can't very well argue with that, can we? People do like to hear good news, and they are far more likely to welcome us if we bring good news, than if we come to their places of business or their homes and spread gloom. There's quite enough bad news in day-to-day living without salespeople adding to the rising tide.

We can't argue with the rule that says sell happiness, not misery, so we won't; we'll just break it now and then.

Why? Why should we want to sell negatively when it is so much more pleasant – and in most cases, much more effective – to sell positively? Well, let's look at the old Benefit motive for buying, that tried and tested and true bastion of all sales training for the last three-quarters of a century. We were all taught to sell benefits because, we were told, benefits are the only reasons that people buy anything at all.

Very nearly correct. Not one hundred per cent right, but nearly right. People do buy benefits, of course they do; it isn't necessary to stress this obvious truth. The problem is that an undue emphasis on the benefit idea in selling can obscure an equally important truth, and that is that people don't buy only to gain benefits; they also buy to avoid *losses*.

If this is true, and a moment's reflection by any advanced salesperson will show the truth of it, then there are times when we have to sell the loss idea instead of the benefit idea – and when we do this we are selling *negatively*.

'But surely,' the thinking salesperson says, 'the benefit and the loss ideas are merely two sides of the same coin?' Yes, they are, and it would seem that in a sales presentation one should be as effective as the other, and in fact this is often the case. The main reason for emphasising the bad news instead of the good news is when we find a customer so locked into his present buying habits that the good news doesn't work on him. We have discussed this problem already in other sections in these pages; it is one of the most difficult selling situations we face.

A fib that we sales trainers tend to tell you is that people usually have very strong and cogent reasons not to buy your products. Sometimes, yes, but the truth is that very often, you won't buy from me not because you have a powerful reason to buy from your present supplier, but because there really seems no reason to change to a new one.

You can prove this to yourself in a very simple way. Walk around your home and look at the things you buy regularly; the cornflakes in your kitchen, the oil in your car, the gin in your drinks cabinet. You have been buying the same brand for years. Why? Well, it works for you, it does the job you bought it to do, you have no complaints about it. But is there any earth-shattering reason to continue buying it? No. Then why do you? Because there is no reason to change, that's why. So over the years you have been building a buying *pattern*. You feel comfortable seeing that brand name on your towels, you are used to that pen, you know where to find the sports pages in that daily paper. So why change?

In this situation it is often not enough to give you the benefits of the new product. They won't make you change from the old product – after all, the old product gives you benefits too, and perhaps they are very similar to those we claim for our new product. So instead of trying to excite the customer with the good things that *will* happen if he changes over, we horrify him with the awful things that *are* happening now or that *can* happen soon.

Below are some examples of selling positively and negatively. As you read them you will probably prefer the feelings the positive examples engender in you; they are, after all, the glad tidings. You may not like the feelings engendered by the negative examples. Good! That means they are working. They are meant to unsettle the customer, to make her uncomfortable, to force her to want to change. See what you think:

This plan will augment your pension fund and give you a second income when you retire.	Seven out of ten people have to keep working after retirement, sometimes in a menial job. You must avoid that, no matter what it costs you.
This small additional premium means that you have complete protection against civil riots; that means real peace of mind for you.	It's a little hard to pay house insurance for twenty years and then find they won't pay out when a mob breaks down your front wall.
This heavy-duty gear oil will keep your truck gearboxes cool in the toughest conditions, giving you extra life for the gears. The product will pay for itself time and time again.	The new contract means that your trucks will be coming out of the quarry with a full load. The gears will be taking a terrible pounding, and without the extra protection it could cost you a fortune in parts and downtime.
Our guarantee that we will take back any chocolate bars which are time-expired means that your customers are always assured of fresh product, and will buy from you with confidence.	If you have to discard one chocolate bar in ten, you are losing most of your profit. Also, think what your customers would feel about your store if they found stale, discoloured chocolate when they opened the packet.

The left-hand examples were more pleasant reading, weren't they? Always nice to get good news. The right-hand ones were not so agreeable. They warned about things that disturbed you, that made you feel apprehensive and alarmed. They were the grit in the oyster shell, the thorn under the saddle, the stone in the shoe. You wanted to do something to get rid of them.

And that is why we sometimes have to break the rule which says sell positively, give the good news, make the customer happy about your product.

You are certainly intelligent and perceptive enough to notice that the sections we have covered so far do not fit into watertight compartments, that there is a fair amount of overlapping in the suggestions I have made, and this section is no exception. Round about now the old, tired spectre of high-pressure selling will probably raise its head, although you would have thought that we had disposed of it for good in earlier sections. Very well, let's pick over its bones for the last time and then bury it for ever. It is true that when we talk about losses rather than benefits, we are walking a fine line between negative selling and high pressure. We can be accused of knocking the opposition, since we are talking about what awful things could happen with the other product. Perhaps it would help you to use a thought which helped me when I was selling negatively, that is, telling the customer what could happen or was happening from his use of other products. It went like this.

Here I was, sitting in the customer's office and giving my sales presentation. It would seem that there were only two people in the room, the customer and me, but no; right behind me and breathing down my neck was the salesman of the opposition company. He wasn't visible, but he was there, and he was listening to every word I said. In this imagined scene, he was allowed to open his mouth and challenge me only if he caught me out in a lie. If he could prove the lie, then I would have to hand the sale over to him and leave. If he couldn't prove that I was lying when I was giving the bad news about his product, then he had to keep his mouth shut and watch me win the customer over to my product.

This may seem like a rather childish game to be playing in

the serious world of competitive selling, but it kept me honest and stopped me from ever being accused of high-pressure selling. Try it the next time you are selling negatively. There you are and your competitor is at your elbow, present but invisible, and eager to catch you out in the slightest misrepresentation. Keep his mouth shut by staying with provable facts, and you may be astonished at the powerful sales talk you will be able to give.

Break the rule, and get *positive* results from selling *negatively*.

Chapter 18

IF AT FIRST YOU DON'T SUCCEED, *DON'T* TRY, TRY, TRY AGAIN

Perseverance, the rule says. Nothing worthwhile is ever easy, so don't expect that sales are going to fall into your lap on the first or second call. Keep calling. This doesn't mean, the rule is quick to warn us, that we must be guilty of undue persistence; none of this 'hanging around until they call the police and have you thrown out' attitude. Nevertheless it is the salesperson who perseveres who gets the order eventually, so don't flit from flower to flower like a butterfly, looking for the easy pickings; if at first you don't succeed, as the old saying goes, try, try, try again.

Nothing wrong with that rule, and as advanced salespeople, you and I have proved its worth time and time again. Is there any situation where it could, and should, be broken? Yes, there is.

Have you ever thought of your job in selling as a pooling of resources between you and your company? The company brings to the venture the product range, the research and development expertise, the marketing thrust, and the before-and after-sales service. You bring three things: your attitude, your talent and your time. It is the last of these which concerns us at the moment.

Take a puppy for a walk in the woods and when he finds a hole made by a small forest animal, he will dig frantically until he is exhausted, even when it is obvious that the hole is empty. An older dog will dig for a moment, sniff, dig some more – and then move from the empty hole and look for another one.

The brand-new salesperson, full of enthusiasm in the search for new prospects, digs away at a possible prospect until he, his manager and the prospect are all exhausted. The more experienced salesperson digs at the hole, sniffs, and goes off to look for a hole with more promise.

We have discussed potential and its importance in a previous section, and it is time to take another look at it, except that now we are going to team potential up with another concept, that of probability. Let us look at four customers, Messrs North, South, East and West. Preliminary investigation, the first sniff at the hole, has indicated that as far as potential is concerned – that is, the ability to buy and the capacity to use our product – the situation is as follows:

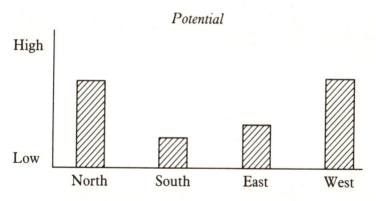

At first sight it seems obvious that North and West are the ones to hit, with all our resources, as often as we can. South and East, with their limited capacity to absorb our products, are hardly worth a second glance.

All right so far, but now we add an additional aspect to our chart: the chances that they will eventually buy from us, or the probability concept. Now it looks like this:

Potential and probability

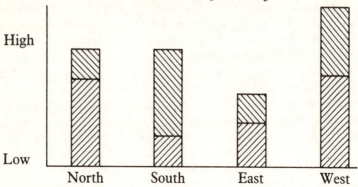

Now the picture looks very different. North has a good potential and they could be big buyers. Trouble is that because of one thing or another, the chances of getting in there are not very high. This does *not* mean that we will give up on them and walk away; oh, no. What it does mean is that we shall be doing a lot of sniffing before we do much digging.

South? Not a big potential, but the chances of selling are good. We shall certainly call and sell here. Always remembering the horror story of the lawnmower repair shop in Chapter 16, so that we don't waste too much time on him, we will call and gather in what limited sheaves are available from his harvest. Call frequency must be carefully monitored so as to keep the profitability of the calls in the black, and so long as we watch this, then by all means call.

All we need to do with East is identify him as quickly as possible and, having done so, turn our backs on him and hope that the opposition goes after him and gets him as a customer. Small buying potential, slim possibility of selling to him – avoid him like typhoid.

West of course needs no explanation, merely a candle lit to the patron saint of salespeople. High capacity, excellent chance of selling to him. Call and call and call again, and sell and sell and sell again.

So we see that the rule which says, try, try, try again is valid only in certain very well defined circumstances. As advanced salespeople, we should be aware of these circumstances, and when they do not apply we must be prepared to break the rule.

What is the difference between perseverance and persistence? Reference books give them as synonyms for each other, but in the vocabulary of salesmanship they are very different animals. Genuine perseverance is always acceptable; undue persistence is not. Later on, in another chapter, we shall be looking at the difference between the two; it all has to do with the *reason* for the call. Right now, let us look at the case of a salesman who called on a customer who very much wanted to buy what the salesman sold. This is the dream of all of us, isn't it? That someone will phone and say, 'I know your product and I need it; please come and see me right away.'

In this true case the salesman made his call on the prospective customer, did not sell him anything, and did not call again for a full year. This is what happened. The product was architects' drawing tables, those high-tech, fully adjustable and very ingenious gadgets at which draughtsmen stand and do their stuff. This particular table was top of the line, up-market, and probably the best of its kind in the world. Well, the office manager greeted the salesman warmly and said he knew the product well, having worked with one of them in his previous job as a draughtsman. Now that he was manager of his own department he wanted all of his people to have the best, and he needed five tables for the new staff he had hired. Things were going well in the call until the price came up, whereupon the manager almost burst into tears. He said in shocked tones, 'Oh, Lord! I had no idea they were as expensive as that. I can't buy them.'

Our salesman didn't let that stop him of course, and he went into the reasons which made the tables, high priced as they were, such a good buy. The manager shook his head and put up his hands. 'No, you don't understand. I'm not haggling, and I'm not saying they are too expensive. They are marvellous tables and I love them, but I have been given a budget for equipment expenditure, and I have been told that it is no good going back and doing an Oliver Twist, because there simply isn't any more. Now, I must have five tables because I have five new people. With the money I have I could buy three and a half of your tables. What can I do?'

Well, you are an advanced salesperson, so what would you

[113]

advise? He can't get another penny from his management and he must have five tables by next week. I said that the salesman walked out with no order and diarised to call again in a year's time. What he did was give the office manager the address of a place which sold used equipment for drawing offices. He said, 'Why not get five used tables and live with them for the rest of the year. This will give you a surplus on your budget. Then explain to your management what you are doing, and from this very moment warn them that next year you will be buying the very best tables available for your people. You might give the news to your draughtsmen, too – give them something to look forward to.'

Perhaps you would have handled it differently and possibly even better than this salesman did, but that isn't the point. The point is that the salesman saw this customer as a high-potential/low-probability prospect, and acted accordingly.

As old dogs, we push our noses into every rabbit hole and give a good sniff. When we realise that the hole is empty *at this time* we move on, leaving the puppies digging their hearts out at an empty hole. To run this analogy threadbare, on the next walk through the forest we would certainly take a passing sniff at the hole in case the situation had changed since last time, but eventually we would realise that the rabbits had left it for ever, and we would stop wasting time on it. Plenty of other holes with fresh rabbit scent in them; go for them.

Try, try, try again? Perhaps, but when we are not sure let's take a look at the potential/probability diagram again, and save ourselves valuable time and effort by breaking the rule.

Chapter 19

DON'T TALK ABOUT YOUR PRODUCT, TALK ABOUT HIS PEOPLE

You are selling a product. Therefore any part of the sales presentation which does not deal with the product is probably a waste of the precious minutes when you are face to face with the prospect. Talk product, the rule says. At the end of the interview you should leave her with a clear idea of the product in her mind. After all, it is the product you want her to buy, so if she remembers nothing else at least let her remember that.

Makes a lot of sense, a rule like that. A salesperson who concentrates on his product during a sales presentation is not going to go very far wrong. We break this rule only when we see something in the customer's situation which is much closer and dearer to his heart. What can this be? The answer is, almost anything. One mistake we make as new salespeople is to believe that the customer is as excited about, and as loyal to, our product as we are. He isn't. Oh, he may like it, he may see that it is doing a better job for him than anything else in the same line, but while for us our product is the biggest thing in business, for our customer a whole world exists in which our salt-glaze piping or washable wallpaper or hypo-allergenic mascara plays no part at all.

And a part of that world is the customer's *people*. These people can be his own staff, his customers, his co-workers, his management or even, in the case of personal selling, his family.

Here are some extracts from sales talks; notice that the emphasis in all of them is on *people*, with the product hardly mentioned:

Showing a copying machine to the chief of the typing department, the saleswoman noticed how well the staff got on with each other; the attitude and atmosphere in the office was friendly, relaxed and cheerful. The chief obviously got on well with her staff and thought a lot of them.

'I must comment on the high standard of morale in your group, Ms Williams. It must make for very pleasant working conditions.'

'Yes, they're a good team. Hand-picked by me, all of them. I believe that a happy ship is an effective ship.'

'Can't argue with that, which makes my job here today easier, because my machine will help to *keep* your team happy.'

'Your copier will make people happy? Oh, come on. I see that it's a good machine, but our present machine was a good one in its day, and it didn't exactly send my women into transports of ecstacy!'

'I mean it. As you know, all these copiers use a toner. Tell me, how many times have you ruined a pair of tights by getting a single drop of the toner on them?'

'Oh, don't talk about it. We have all suffered that way.'

'Right! But with this machine the operators don't even have to open the bottle. They turn it upside down, still sealed, and drop it into place, and only when they close the lid does the spike pierce the bottle top. I tell you, the tights manufacturers hate this machine! As you say, Ms Williams, you have a happy ship. Take the copier aboard and you'll keep it happy!'

The *product* was mentioned only to show what it did for *people*.

To the transport manager of a foundry:

'Tell me, do you have trouble getting and keeping good drivers?'

'M-m. Always a problem; they put on their jackets and walk across the road for no reason at all.'

'And usually at the worst possible time, I suppose. Do you know that drivers fight to drive our trucks?'

'What do you mean?'

'We had an independent survey done. Here you are, there are the results. Do you see that our Long Haul series, from the

LH 70 right up to the LH 220, was the most popular truck among the drivers interviewed by as much as twenty-eight per cent.'

'M-m. Impressive, if it's true.'

'By all means phone the research people; here's the number. What this means is that drivers tend to stay with the company that runs our trucks.'

In this actual case history, the reasons that the drivers gave for their preference were comfort and ease of parking in restricted places. But do you notice that the salesman didn't even mention that in his talk? He saw that the transport manager didn't really have the interests of the drivers at heart, what he wanted was something which would make his job easy, and in this case it was the fact that he might possibly have less bother having to keep on hiring new drivers to replace the ones who left. The truck was especially comfortable because of a most advanced design of driver's seat, which could be adjusted electrically while on the road; the salesman didn't even mention the seat. The truck was easy to park because of excellent all-round visibility and the variable power-assisted steering; the salesman ignored the steering. He played down the product and played up the people angle, and his sales talk hit the spot.

Selling washing powder to a chain-store buyer:

'I think you'll agree that you could walk around a self-service store blindfolded and you would know when you got to the detergent shelves because you would smell the powder. No matter how carefully they pack those cardboard boxes, no matter what glue they use on them, the damned powder gets out somehow. So your customer sticks the box into her trolley right on top of the cauliflower she has just picked up at your vegetable department. Now your packer at the checkout counter separates the detergent from the foodstuffs and even puts it into a bag by itself, but the damage has already been done, and when she cooks her cauliflower cheese, it smells like washing powder, and she can't wait to give you a hard time when she comes back – that is, if she ever does.'

'So?'

'So it can't happen with our detergent. The packet is lined

with two-millimetre polyethylene sheeting, heat-sealed. So it isn't necessary even to put it in a separate bag, which is convenient, because how many of your customers bring more than one bag? And they certainly don't like buying an extra bag from you. Result? Happy customer, happy packer, happy you – and when you sign this order, happy me.'

There will be many times when we obey the sound and logical rule that we talk *product*. There are many times when a detailed explanation of the product is essential, and we would not be professionals if we were not ready to deliver that sort of presentation. Sometimes though, it pays to push the product aside and talk about the *people* who will buy, use, pack, count, repair, drive, operate, wear or eat the product. People, after all, are much more interesting than products.

Chapter 20

ENCOURAGE OBJECTIONS!

The rule says, try to avoid getting a direct objection from the customer. Do your best not to get into a situation where he says, 'No, your specifications are wrong for my conditions,' or, 'I wouldn't dream of buying roofing which is not hot-dip galvanised,' or, 'That design is too boring – it won't make an attractive package.'

The rule says that once the customer has actually come out with the objection, has articulated it in open court, as it were, it is a concrete thing. He has put it into words and he is now committed to it. It is his contribution to the sales interview and, in a way, he is proud of it. You have come along with this polished and fluent sales presentation and you are holding forth; the platform is yours. He wants to have an active part in the scene, so he searches for something which will stop you dead in your tracks. What can he say? Ah! 'Sorry, but this company has never used billboard advertising; it simply does not work for our industry.'

Now you have a problem. He has put up his barrier to buying and you have the job of painstakingly dismantling it before you can go on. You were even warned, if you remember your early sales training, that if you did have an irrefutable and infallible answer to his objection, the worst thing you could do would be to smash through it as though it was a trivial or petty thing, of no importance or relevance in a serious discussion. That way you could easily antagonise the customer to the extent where he thinks (or even says outright): 'All right; you may be very clever, but the decision is mine and

I say no!' He pushes reason and logic aside, because we have belittled his objection.

So, much better to voice your presentation in such a way that you avoid objections. In that way they will stay faint, blurred and vague, whereas if he actually puts them into words they will become strong, clear and specific.

It's a good rule which has worked many hundreds of times for you and me. We break it with our eyes open and a clear idea of what we are doing and why.

The truth is that sometimes we *want* the customer to raise her objections. Sometimes the only way we will ever sell to her is by getting her to say, 'I won't buy from you!' How can this be? Well, it all goes back to an outright lie which we were told when we first became salespeople. We have spared a passing glance at this earlier in this manual – as we see, the sections flow into each other, there are few watertight compartments – but now we have to face it head-on. The axiom goes like this:

The hardest thing to handle in selling is the strong objection.

It's a lie.

We have all been faced with tough objections and many times we have been unable to overcome them; they have been too strong, too cogent and too valid for us and we have failed. But we have also had those objections which at first seemed to be insurmountable, which made us feel that this was it, no sale today. Yet we bit on the bullet and soldiered on and hey – what we said just then seemed to make sense to the customer and look, she is nodding her head and we are in business again.

The strong objection is not the hardest thing to handle in selling; the hardest thing to handle in selling is when the customer won't *talk*! When he won't give you his reason for not buying, how in the world are you going to overcome it?

Before we go any further, let's be clear about something. I am not saying that we should welcome objections and be unhappy when they don't appear. That would be like urging the cross-country runner to welcome the mudhole and the rocks and feel deprived when he doesn't have to fight his way through them. All I say is that if the listener does have what seem to him to be strong and logical reasons for not buying and he does not voice them, then we have exactly nought per cent chance of selling to him.

No salesperson in his right mind loves getting objections. We would be less than human if we didn't worry sometimes about getting them, and this section is concerned with this worry. There is a way to change your attitude towards the strong objections which you are faced with throughout your selling career. If you go into an important interview thinking, 'Oh, hell, I hope he doesn't hit me with a tough one today,' then what we are about to do will help you. Come with me, because when we have finished what we are about to do, I promise you that you will never worry about objections again. I don't say that you will always be able to overcome them, that would be an idiotic promise. I do say that your *attitude* towards that terrifying word '*no*' will change for the better, and if your attitude is right you stand a much better chance of handling the objection competently. Here we go; this exercise will cost you a few pence in money and a few hours in time, although it will be two months before you see any dramatic change in yourself.

First, buy yourself a small pocket notebook. Yes, I know that you already have one, but get another one for the other pocket. If you care to lash out then get one with a pencil fitted into the spine. You now have all the equipment you need for your project. Your first step, then:

Collect objections

For the next thirty days, deliberately go out of your way to get your customers to give you their reasons for not buying.

You will be doing exactly what you normally do, that is, making your calls and giving your presentations and doing your very best to sell your products. The difference will be that you will be taking the most careful note of anything that anyone says which in any way resembles a reason not to buy. When you fail to sell and an objection is not forthcoming, drag it out of the customer. Say something like, 'I respect your decision not to buy at this time, but it would help me tremendously if you could tell me what has made you say no.'

When he realises that you are not going to give him a hard time or high-pressure him, he will usually relax and come out with the real reason.

Good; you didn't make the sale, but you have what you wanted. Incidentally, the fact that you made no sale then doesn't stop you from going back at a later date and saying, 'Since we last talked, I have been thinking about what you said, and . . . ', and you are in there pitching again. Now, the moment you leave that customer's place of business and *before* you make your next call, get out your little notebook and write down the customer's objection, *exactly as he said it*. Don't paraphrase it or shorten it or turn it into your own words; put it down, word for word.

You should also put down the objections which you were able to overcome. This is important, because although you were successful with them this time it doesn't mean that you will beat them next time. The idea here is to include every single objection you can get, so stick them down.

Well, at the end of that first month you will have a book full of reasons for *not* buying what you sell, and you might think that it would make rather doleful reading. Oddly enough, it won't depress you at all. Instead of thinking, 'Oh, Lord, with all these reasons for not buying, why should anybody buy?' you will have the feeling that now you've got them *all* in your little book, and you are on your way to defeating them. It's an extraordinary feeling and I can't explain it better than that, but I assure you, at the end of that first month you will feel better already (and you haven't yet lifted a finger to overcome the objections!). Next step is to sit down with the notebook and go through the objections, one by one. First thing to do:

Throw out the easy ones

Put a line through those objections which don't worry you. You get them thrown at you, sure, but most of the time you have no trouble answering them in such a way that they wither and die. You had to record them when they were said, because you were putting down everything, but now you are being selective, so you can throw them out.

Throw out the one-offs

You will get a few real odd-ball objections and it may be that you can't think of a single way to handle them. 'I'm sorry but my manager is Turkish and he won't let me buy from a company such as yours, which has extensive interests in Greece.' This may be beyond your power to handle, but why bother? It won't come up more than once in ten years, so put a line through it.

Classify what's left

Right, now you are left with the tough, common objections. Go through them carefully, and you will find that although they are all put in different words, they fit into a few simple categories. For instance:

'I'm not paying more than £6.50 for word-processor ribbons.'
'Your opposition gives me ninety days free of interest.'
'That price is too rich for my blood.'
'The readers in this area won't pay that much for a paperback romance.'
'I don't get enough discount from you people.'

Those objections are all put in different words, but they are all connected with the price problem; they all fit into one *category*.

Similarly you will find other objections which fit into a category having to do with the manufacture of the product – the way it is made, the materials it is made from, its size or weight or flexibility or waterproofing or stress resistance or – you name it. These can all be classified under specifications, and you have a new category.

One more category is worth discussing here. (You will find others depending on what you are selling, but this one is universal.) We could call this one *personal*. For some examples of this category, take the pharmaceutical business:

- Some doctors will not look at clinical trials of products when they are done in certain countries; they don't trust them.

[123]

- You get doctors who dislike what they call 'shotgun therapy', which means that the treatment is a combination of several drugs intended to treat different diseases.

- There are doctors who will not prescribe any sort of 'tonic' and who are insulted when you suggest that they do.

- Many doctors will not prescribe anything at all for a woman in the first three months of pregnancy, and it requires a very special approach before they will even listen to you on this subject.

Now all of these can be put into the 'personal' category because they are all personal likes and dislikes of the customer. I have had salespeople who, when I mentioned this category, said immediately, 'Never mind calling it "personal"; what you have there is a set of prejudices, and that's what I'll call it.' Okay by me.

Now, once you have done all this, and it takes much less time than you may think, you will have made an incredible discovery. It is a discovery which, by itself, with no attempt yet to handle or overcome the objections, will change your attitude towards anyone who says, 'Sorry, no sale.' Look at what you have done; instead of a book full of objections you have a few – very few – *types* of objections to buying your product. When I say 'very few' I am tempted to tell you just how few it will be. I'm not going to tell you because until you do this exercise you won't believe me. You face sales resistance day after day, don't you? You get what seems to be a long list of solid, logical arguments against buying. So if I tried to tell you that it is highly probable that there are no more than two or three *types* or *categories* of objections, you would think that I was living in a dream world. So I won't tell you. Do it yourself, carry out the exercise exactly as I have put it down, and see what you end up with. It will take you one month to collect the objections and one evening to do everything else we have discussed so far.

Well, that is all very well, but we haven't yet done anything about *handling* these categories of objections. What's the next step?

Look for solutions

There are reasons not to buy your products? Then there are reasons to buy them, too. The next month is spent in searching for these reasons. Where do we find them? Many places.

• The product itself

When did you last look at what you sell? It's not such a silly question as it sounds. We get so used to the things we sell that sometimes we forget the finer points. Try to look at your product – and I mean actually and physically; put it down and walk around it – with the eyes of someone who has never seen it before. Why was it designed exactly like that and not another way? When you have done that, go back to your product literature; gather together everything that has ever been put on paper about the product. There are catalogues, manuals, diagrams, charts, test results, photographs – stuff that we haven't even opened, much less read, for ages. Often the answers we want are right there.

• The boffins

If you sell a highly technical range of products it is likely that you have technical people – engineers, mechanics, repair-men – who deal with the nuts and bolts of the product every day. They don't look at the product from the sales point of view, but perhaps that's a good thing. You may be able to get a new slant on what you sell from the people who make it or assemble it or fix it. You will probably find that they are delighted to help you.

• Your customers

Certainly, your customers; why not? Sometimes when someone says, 'I would never buy that product,' we forget that someone has bought it, is continuing to buy it, is completely ecstatic about it and would never consider buying anything else. Why? Is he stupid, this regular customer of ours? No, of course he is not. So why not ask him? 'Mr Green, those printing plates are doing a really good job for you. You know, I sometimes get people who like the look of them but who hesitate to buy because they are so much thinner than the normal plates. Yet this obviously doesn't bother you. Why not?'

'Well, I'll tell you frankly that it did worry me a little in the beginning. My printers were used to the thicker plates and I didn't want to confuse them. But you know, when we finally did make the change we found that . . . '

Or: 'Ms White, I know that you have to be very careful with your budget. You have bought our oils and acrylics for your students for three years now, and you know very well that there are cheaper paints on the market. Why do you spend the extra few pounds when you could buy cheaper?'

'Do you remember last year when I didn't give you my usual order? Well, after one month I came back to you, didn't I? I decided to try the cheaper colours. I must admit I liked the lower price, but my students complained all through that month. It was a real relief to get back to your paints.'

What would answers like that do to your morale and your attitude towards objections? You know what it would do – it would turbo-charge you! We don't use our customers nearly enough, you know, and don't ever think that they mind our asking them that sort of question; the fact is that they love it. They are so used to our coming in and talking with all the authority of the expert that it is refreshing for them to find that we are actually asking them for their opinions and advice. Do it, and remember that whenever you get an 'I won't buy because – ' you have had many 'I did buy because – '

● **Your colleagues**
One of the most useful things I ever did with my fellow salespeople was to sit around in a small group – and I mean really small, say four or five – and bounce objections around. The resistance to buying which you fear so much turns out to be not a big problem to Henry over there because he seems to have an answer which often works for him. But Henry is really bothered when someone says, 'No, I won't buy because . . . ' Well, Richard doesn't find that one so hard, but who can help Richard with *this* one? Well, Janet got that one yesterday, and she tried . . .

This sort of informal brainstorming can be very rewarding. Even if no magical answers are forthcoming it helps the team to realise that they are not alone out there and that others are having the same sort of problems and are coping with them in some way or other.

Well, then; after two months what have you got? You have a few, a very few, types of reasons why people don't buy your products. You have answers to them. These answers won't be infallible, they won't all work on all people, but they are valid, logical and sound – and they give you something to say, instead of reacting to the objection as though the customer had just sentenced you to being burnt at the stake. Remember, I promised that this method would change your *attitude* towards sales resistance.

And now we are ready for the last step which is simply to:

Put them to work

Sooner or later I meet everyone I know at airports, and I have got used to hearing, 'Hey, Michael!' yelled across a transit lounge. It happened again recently and the yeller turned out to be a salesman who had attended a sales clinic where we had gone quite deeply into the problems of handling objections. He couldn't wait to tell me that he had tried my method. 'And what do you know, Michael, it worked!'

I said, not all that pleased at the note of disbelief in his voice, 'Well, I told you it would work.'

'Yes, I know, but I thought it was like so many of the things they tell you in sales training.'

'Thanks very much.'

He was too eager to tell me all about it to be put off by my reaction to being classed with whoever 'they' might be. He said, 'I didn't think it would work but I was getting to the stage where I dreaded the thought of getting one more objection, and it was affecting my sales presentation.'

This is what happens, of course. We worry so much about the listener saying 'No' that we can't concentrate on giving our best presentation, which in turn makes the listener say 'No', which makes us worry even more . . .

[127]

'Anyway, I bought the notebook and I put down all the objections and went through the whole business of classifying them and throwing out the easy ones – '

They were calling my flight. I said, 'Yes, so what happened?'

'Well then, I went out and put it to work, and the very first person I called on said, "No, I don't want anything which contains synthetic resins." Well, I said to myself, okay, that's the Specification category. I had a couple of answers to that and I used them.'

'And?' I had my boarding pass in my hand.

'And they worked! And then an incredible thing happened! I waited for him to give me another objection and he didn't!' He grasped my arm; he wasn't going to allow me to get on that plane until I had heard the whole story. 'Do you know how I felt, Michael? I felt like saying, "Hey, come on; you can do better than that, sir. You're not trying hard enough!" '

I said, 'Wonderful!' and made it through the gate in time. It *was* wonderful. Here was someone who had feared the thought of a prospective customer saying, 'I won't buy because . . . ' and who had changed his attitude to the extent that he now felt that the man hadn't put up a decent fight. Wonderful, indeed.

As an advanced salesperson you would scoff at a claim that any method will overcome all possible objections. What we have been doing here is examining a way to change our attitude, because simply by doing this we gain a valuable psychological advantage. If you are bothered, worried, concerned and depressed when you are faced with an objection – and it is something which is very difficult to conceal – then the customer immediately occupies the high ground in your verbal duel. If, on the other hand, it seems to him that the objection does not in any way discompose you, it has the effect of diminishing its validity and strength. The reaction of the customer will often be: 'It doesn't seem to disturb this salesman; he seems quite at ease about it. Perhaps I have been concerned over nothing?'

Oh, it works; it works very well indeed. But in order to make it work we have to break a rule, and get the customer to raise objections.

Chapter 21

DON'T BOTHER TO CLOSE THE SALE

I've said it myself to thousands of sales trainees: 'If you don't try to close the sale, you aren't a salesperson at all; you are merely an explainer, a demonstrator, an exhibitor of products. Only when you get into a closing mode, can you call yourself a salesman.'

The rule is, always make a determined effort to get action from the customer. Use whatever technique you please, do whatever it takes, but *try to close*. Nothing happens until you do.

It's another of those fundamental rules in selling which seem to be so obvious and self-explanatory that they hardly need to be mentioned, let alone discussed or examined. Yet the interesting thing is that the more experienced a salesperson gets, the more advanced and successful he becomes, the less he bothers about what is popularly known in sales training as The Closing Step. If you think about it you will realise that when you are really selling well, at the top of your capability, you don't ever say to yourself, 'Now he's about ready for the closing step. Now, of all the techniques they taught me in my first selling seminar, which will be the best one to use here? There were fourteen of them, as I remember; which one will best tie him up tight?'

You don't think like that these days. Way back when you were a young hopeful, yes; then it was comforting to have all those options to use, and if the first one didn't work, why, there were thirteen more to choose from. These days you don't give the fourteen a thought, and in fact it is doubtful whether you could name more than three of them without digging around in your attic or garage and finding the manual from the first sales course under a pile of newspapers.

So you don't really think about closing the sale at all. What happens in the sales call as you are talking to your customer (or a hundred times better, talking *with* your customer, so that the call is truly a conversation and not a monologue), is that you reach a point where you know that he is going to buy. He may not say 'Yes'; he may not say or do anything at all, but you know without a shadow of doubt that you have sold him.

The interesting thing is that this knowledge may not come at the end of the presentation, where it would be logical; it can happen anywhere. Think back over the years and you will agree that there have been times when you have had this realisation of success a minute or two after you have started selling – you *knew* that the outcome would be a successful sale. Your presentation is not finished – heavens, it has barely started – but he is going to buy. It is one of the most marvellous feelings a salesperson can ever have, and the point is that it happens without your having deliberately tried to 'close the sale' at all.

So the rule which says that we should make a real and deliberate effort to close the sale, that unless we do we are not really selling, may be a good one for the tenderfoot salesperson, but for us advanced people it is one which we break almost as a matter of course.

If you are still doubtful about breaking this rule – and if you are, I don't blame you, because it is hard to give up some of the old shibboleths – then think for a moment. When all the undergrowth is cleared away, why does anybody buy anything? The answer is that they buy because they believe that the things will improve their situation in some way or another. Whether the purchase is a box of matches or a cottage by the sea, they were bought because by owning them we are able to do something which we were not able to do before. I'm sorry to labour this self-evident point, but we have to realise that people don't buy because of any 'closing technique'; they buy because in their mental computers the 'go' factors outweigh the 'no-go' factors, and the decision is made in that way. If, on the other hand, the 'no-go' factors outweigh the 'go' factors, then the sale is lost to the salesman, *and no closing technique will change that.*

What I am slowly getting around to, and you are quite intelligent enough to realise it, is that the advanced salesperson relies much more on the power of his sales argument than on any techniques.

I once worked with a salesman who impressed me with the ease with which he seemed to be able to persuade customers to buy from him. There were no dramatics, no smooth line of talk; he didn't seem to stick to any logical theme in his presentation and he certainly didn't make a point of getting any closing action. I told him that he seemed to sell painlessly and without any trauma, and he smiled. He said, 'Well, Michael, the thing is that I'm not very good at sales talks, so the only thing I can do is make my proposal so attractive that the customer buys anyway.'

An interesting way of looking at it! What he meant was that people buy because of how the product, plan, service or idea will change their lives, in small or big ways, and when this is pointed out to them logically and cogently, they will buy. *They 'close the sale' themselves.*

Let me show you something I am not proud of. When I first started training salespeople I used the old idea of a sales presentation being composed of a series of steps. Nothing extraordinary or original about this; it has been done for ages by many trainers. I used to show the sales presentation as looking something like this:

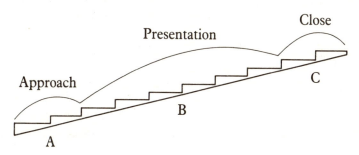

Fig. 1

[131]

In this figure, 'A' was the preliminary section. This was where you, as it were, prepared the customer for the presentation, you set the stage, you created the climate where he was in a listening mood.

'B' was the main body of the talk, and I would point out that it was the largest and longest part of the sale, because here was where you made your benefit claims, supported these with proof, answered all questions and handled sales resistance.

'C' was the action step. This was where you got him to say 'Yes,' to sign the order and do whatever was necessary to close the sale.

Well, looking at the diagram and my explanation of it, you may wonder why I should say I'm not proud of it. It seems to be a reasonable way to describe a typical sales presentation; not very dramatic or exciting, perhaps, but perfectly valid.

I used to think so, too; in fact, I used the step diagram to show that the 'C' section must never occupy too much of the sales talk, that it should never look like this:

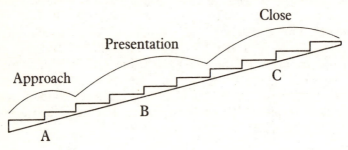

Fig. 2

I said that this was a diagram of a very poor sales talk, because what had happened here was that the salesman had leapt into the closing stage without doing a proper job in the body of the sale. For the diagram to look like this meant that something had been left out of the 'B' section. Specific benefits or losses have not been properly explained, back-up evidence has not been brought out, the customer's reactions have not been noted and built on – something is missing. So from the end of this incomplete 'B' section, lukewarm, the salesman has tried to drag the customer through the closing step before he is ready. You could call that a diagram of a high-pressure sales talk.

But again, you might feel that what is laid out here is a perfectly reasonable explanation of what goes on in a sales talk, so what have I got against it? After all, I used it for years, didn't I? Yes, I did, and in fact I still use it – for my brand-new salespeople; for you, the advanced salespeople, it isn't good enough. The truth is that for you, while Fig. 2 is obviously wrong, even Fig. 1 is wrong. Take section 'A', for instance. After all your experience in selling, you are confident enough to move quickly into the body of your sales presentation without a lot of preliminary yacking about the weather, the state of business and the progress of the Chunnel. You know that this isn't very professional anyway, and you have the skill to carry your customer along with you almost from the moment you shake his hand. So your 'A' is much shorter than Fig. 1:

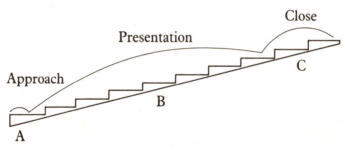

Fig. 3

Much more professional that way, isn't it? Remember that people like to deal with busy, successful people, and if you have all the time in the world to spend in section 'A', then you don't look very busy and you won't seem very successful.

But section 'C' is wrong, too, and so we have one more change to make in the diagram. Our experience, based on thousands of sales calls, allows us to watch and listen to the customer as the presentation progresses. We see that, yes, he has moved from the attitude of 'I see no reason to buy', through 'This does sound interesting' to 'I must have this.' *All this happens in the 'B' section*, the body of the sales presentation. The 'C' section, if it exists at all, consists of your saying something like, 'Let's start with six units, then,' or, 'Can you give me an order number for this?' or simply turning the order pad round with the pen resting on it. If you insist on calling those three 'closing techniques', I shan't argue with you, although they hardly deserve the name. The point is that for the advanced salesperson the diagram should actually look like this:

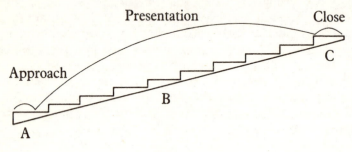

Fig. 4

Even here I am half inclined to cross the 'C' out entirely, but let's leave it in for the purists.

The point, and the purpose of this chapter, is that when we are experienced, skilful and advanced enough, our presentations are good enough so that we truly don't 'close' the customer. Somewhere in section 'B' the 'go' factors outweigh the 'no-go' factors in his mind, and when that happens there is no way that you *can't* sell to him, because if you try to stop him buying he will want to kill you.

Break the rule about closing the sale and sell the professional way.

Chapter 22

'WHY I HATE SALESPEOPLE!'
or,
THE RULES WE *NEVER* BREAK

I was once shown the results of a survey which a client company of mine had had done for them by an independent market research outfit. They had interviewed several hundred buyers to find out what the buyers disliked about the salespeople who called on them; in fact, they were trying to find out what salespeople were doing wrong.

For some reason, which I never did discover, the company didn't use the results of the survey; perhaps they thought it was too disheartening or inflammatory. I have never forgotten them, though, because what we are about to examine are some of the rules which we must *never* break, no matter what. You can believe the contents of this chapter, because this is straight from the horse's mouth – this is *your* customer talking to *you*.

To the question, 'What do you dislike about salespeople?' the buyers answered as follows:

'He wastes my time!'
By a large and unhappy majority, this one was the top of the unpops, a real cry from the heart of busy buyers, already behind in their work, having to watch their precious minutes and hours thrown away by over-loquacious salespeople spouting the same, tired, old sales talks they had heard so many times before.

Or at least, that is the impression we gain from the simple and direct complaint, 'He wastes my time.'

Now, I think that when we look at the answers to this survey, we need to do a little mental discounting. You can see, can't you, a buyer who is asked, 'What don't you like about salespeople?' He's rolling his sleeves up, licking his lips and saying to himself, at last! Here is my chance to get back at some of those washouts who barge in here on the hour, every hour. Perhaps it is natural that their answers may be exaggerated a little; however, they would not be wrong. The people surveyed might have been a little more definite and categorical than the question warranted, but they were not lying. What came out was the truth.

I was fascinated by this answer. Was this the worst thing that we did, to waste the customer's time? With the client company's permission, I got in touch with the research organisation that had done the survey, to go further into it, and I found something very interesting. I asked the executive in charge of the survey: 'Does this mean that the salespeople spent too long with the buyer? Should we all shorten our calls, maybe even cut them in half?'

She said, 'No, not at all. What we found was that a salesperson might spend two hours with a buyer, and not waste a single minute of his time; then the next one who calls on that same buyer could spend ten minutes with him – and waste all that ten minutes.'

I knew it. I had always known it. Let's take some examples. Let us say that you will be calling on a buyer tomorrow and that you will, in the course of that call, do one or more of the following things:

- Show him a new application for a product he is already buying from you.

- Help him with a problem, perhaps nothing to do with anything you sell him, which is bothering him.

- Give him news of a new range of products that will soon hit the market and will fit into his business.

- Warn him about proposed legislation that will affect him.

- Show him how to cut a corner in his manufacturing process (which will allow him to use slightly *less* of your product).

[136]

- Give him a copy of a trade magazine with an article of interest to him.

- Check that your products are arriving at his factory in the same condition that they left your factory.

When you shake his hand and leave after that call he is not going to say, 'Damn it, another pedlar wasting my time again.' How long would you have spent with him on that call? Oh, if only all questions were as easy as that one! The answer is: *as long as it takes*. Five minutes or five hours of his available time, and you need never worry that you will be wasting any of it.

Or, you could call and do any one of the following things:

- Give him the identical sales pitch which you gave him last time and which didn't work then.

- Ask him how his fishing trip went.

- Tell him how your fishing trip went.

- Accept his polite, if reluctant, offer to have some coffee, when he isn't having any.

- Ask him, 'Anything for me this week?'

- Ask him, 'Any problems?' (Put like that, vague and woolly, the answer is *always* 'No'.)

When you leave after that call, he will always shake his head and mutter 'Time-waster' and inform his secretary, 'No more salesmen today; I can't afford to waste any more time.'

The difference between the first group of actions and the second is this: in the first you had a *reason* to call, in the second you hadn't. It is truly as simple as that.

When I first took over a sales team as their manager, they must have thought I wasn't very bright, because when I went out into the field with each one of them I would ask, just before we made a call, 'Why are we calling on this customer?' After a blank stare from the salesman, I would get answers like this:

'Because he's on my list.' That's not a reason.

'I call on him every month.' That's not a reason.

'He's a customer of mine.' That's not a reason.

'It's a welding shop. I call on welding shops.' That's not a reason.

'I might as well drop in; it's on my way to a big customer, so it's not as if I was wasting petrol.' That's not a reason.

Make a call because of any of the above and you will be wasting the time of the person you call on.

Once or twice, to my question about why we were calling, I would get the sarcastic response from my salesman, 'Well, I know this sounds silly, but I'm a salesman, and I thought I might just sell him something today.' That's not a reason, either; at least, not a specific enough reason.

Well, eventually my salesmen got the message and realised what I was after with my apparently meaningless question, and I began to get answers like this:

'The opposition has just increased its price by eight per cent. Now's the time to move in and stock this outlet up.' That's a reason.

'I promised to find out the wet-strength of our polyethylene tissues, and I've got the dope for him.' That's a reason.

'He seems to have stopped buying our two-inch masking tape, and he used to love it. I have to find out why.' That's a reason.

'He won't use our dump-bins. I have proof that a dump-bin, properly placed, will increase his sales by up to a third.' That's a reason.

'She has just hired a new clerk. I'd better see that she knows how to use our fax.' That's a reason.

Have a *reason* to call and you will never be accused of wasting his time.

'Oh, it's not as easy as that,' I hear some experienced salespeople say. 'It may be okay for those examples you have dreamed up, but I sell retread tyres to truck companies, and my monthly call is a routine affair, just to find out if he needs any more retreads. When you really get down to it, that's the reason I call, and you can't glamorise it in any way.'

Perhaps not, and I don't pretend that you can find something to talk about on every call that will make the customer jump out of his socks with enthusiasm. But how difficult is it to say or do something – anything – better than the tired old, 'Anything on the spike for me today?' of the eight calls and four orders per day order-picker-upper?

How well you do this is limited only by your own imagination. What about the salespeople who subscribe to trade magazines (the company may already do this) that cater for the special interests of their clients? The salespeople who sell to stores should get the journals which aim at the retail industry. Those who sell to construction companies, to pharmacists, to foundries, to physiotherapists or to farmers can all find magazines which are beamed at these people. Just how difficult is it to say, 'Ms Hooper, I made a copy of the article in this magazine on shin-splints. I thought you might like to read it because of the number of patients you seem to be getting with this problem.' If Ms Hooper hasn't seen the article, it is a fine way to get into the sales presentation. If she *has* read it, then the next question goes something like, 'What did you think of it – are they on the right lines?' Either way, you have a *reason* to call.

There is always something to ask, say or show. Go back through your product literature, your samples, your demonstration kits, your testimonial letters, your comparison tests. One problem, you know, is that we get sick of the sight of our sales aids. We have been working with them for a long time, sometimes for years, and to us they are stale and dull and old. We forget that to other people those stale, dull, old things can be fresh and exciting and new.

'*Have a reason for calling*': gum it on your bathroom mirror, stick it on the flap of your briefcase, write it inside your order-book.

The second complaint from buyers about salespeople was:

'He breaks promises!'

Apparently this was a real irritation, coming as it did after the time-wasting complaint. Under this heading, buyers put remarks like these:

'They promise you the moon in order to make the sale, with no idea of keeping their word.'

'You have to take anything a salesman says with a pinch of salt.'

'She told me that they would keep that pattern for at least ten years, and they stopped making it the year after I bought it.'

'Always remember that what you are hearing is not the truth, it's just a sales talk.'

'There are liars, damned liars, and salesmen.'

'He promised me with his hand on his heart that they would deliver before the end of May. I got it on 21 June.'

Well! Not a very inspiring read, is it? Are we really as bad as all that? Do we advanced salespeople deserve to have accusations like that thrown at us, or are we being tarred with the same brush as a small minority? Let's see.

I suppose that when buyers complain about salesmen breaking promises, the promises are mostly to do with the delivery dates of orders. 'You'll have it by the end of the week for sure,' does often turn out to mean the end of some week or other, but not this one. Whose fault is this? I look back on my salad days in selling and I recall with shame that in order to tie the customer up nice and tight and make the sale a certainty, I would quote a delivery date which in my heart I knew to be – if not impossible – at least, highly unlikely. This is a naughty practice of some salespeople; the thing is that the customer is probably committed to us because when the delivery date does come round, he can't say, 'You haven't delivered on the promised date so I'm cancelling and getting it elsewhere.' By that time it is often too late for him to switch over to another supplier. Very unethical practice, and very short-sighted, because even if he is a captive customer this time, it is doubtful whether he will ever deal with us again.

If you are an advanced salesperson, I know what you are bursting to say at this point: 'Wait a minute! Let's for once stop blaming the poor bloody salesman for everything from acid rain to urban crime.' You will then give me an example like this:

A customer asks for a specific delivery date. As someone who has suffered from delivery foul-ups before, you don't promise anything until you have checked with your factory foreman, warehouse supervisor, despatch manager – who- ever. You are told that there will be no problem, that the order will be ready in good time. You take this information back to your customer, who signs the order on your promise that you will honour the date agreed on.

Three days before the sacred date you are told, 'Oh, by the way, that order for the Armstrong Company. We can't get the orange ink for silk-screening the cartons. Will red do? If it has to be orange, the order will be delayed five days.' You know perfectly well that red will most certainly not do. So you have the delightful job of going back to the customer and giving him the bad news, so that when a market researcher comes round to that buyer and says, 'What do you hate about salesmen?' she gets the answer: 'They break promises!'

That is more or less the example you were going to give, wasn't it? And of course, you are absolutely right. As ad- vanced salespeople, we are walking wounded from the effects of having to take the blame for other people's sins of omission or commission. When you had the choice between Chancellor of the Exchequer and salesperson as a way of making a living, and you chose the latter because you meet a better class of people in selling, you accepted that there would be many times when you had to stand and take it while somebody told you that the next time the flaps on his cornflakes packets were not properly gummed down, he would personally have the top of your skull for an ashtray. All right, we understand that, but it doesn't help us with the delivery problem cited above (no matter whose fault it is) and the broken promise it produced. What can we do?

Here are two salesmen, Clarence and Cuthbert. They have both, in perfectly good faith and with all the assurance in the world from their internal staff, promised their customers delivery on the 20th of the month. Murphy's Law comes into effect and on the 16th they are both given the bad news:

[141]

'Sorry, boys, but we can't deliver until the 24th. Nobody's fault, of course, number three turret lathe has packed up, both toolmakers are off sick, the shipping documents are mislaid and it is a public holiday in Bangladesh. Hope your customer won't be inconvenienced.'

Faced with this, what does Clarence do? He buys chocolates for the switchboard operator and flowers for the receptionist and says, 'If anybody from Purple Promotions PLC wants me, tell them I'm in the space shuttle, I'm in an oxygen tent, I'm having labour pains – anything. Just don't let them speak to me.' That's Clarence, and by ducking the problem he is, of course, compounding it – and breaking a promise.

In the same situation, Cuthbert picks up the phone and says, 'Please get me the buyer at Orange Enterprises PLC.' Or even better, he gets into his car and he goes to see him. This does not solve the problem, of course, but by addressing it without delay, he is at least containing it, not allowing it to multiply, and because he is immediately informing the customer of the delay and the reason for it he is not breaking a promise. In this way, perhaps something can be done; by giving the customer as much advance notice as possible, Cuthbert gives him space to move in. Whatever the situation, the next time Cuthbert calls on that customer, he stands a chance of getting an order, while Clarence has as much chance with his customer as a tadpole in the Gobi desert.

Be very careful of making a promise in the first place, but once made, keep it at all costs. That is a rule we do not break.

The third complaint, and it is a first cousin of the one we have just examined although it deserves a place of its own, was:

'He overclaims!'

Salespeople do it; oh, yes, they do it. They give the cash value of the insurance policy at age 68 and say it is for age 65, they say that the tensile strength is 12,000 lbs per square inch when it is 9,000. They swear that the cure rate for otitis media is 93 per cent when it is actually 81 per cent, they insist that the average life of the backhoe teeth is 300 hours when the fact is that not one has ever lasted longer than 220 hours. A senior

[142]

manager once said to me in extreme irritation: 'Oh, he tells lies, all right; what makes me so furious is that they are such *stupid* lies!'

Overclaiming for one's product is a *stupid* thing to do, because we are certain to be found out eventually, and when it happens it is such a humiliating thing. I think that what has kept me reasonably honest in selling is not so much an elevated personal moral code as a reluctance to put myself in a position where someone can say, 'You told me that, and it was a bare-faced lie.'

A doctor, who had been prescribing the products of a certain drug house for years, suddenly stopped using them altogether. Why? Because the twit of a salesman barged into his office, plonked down a bottle of pills and said, 'This is the answer to all your asthma patients' problems!' The doctor told me this himself, and he was fuming. He said, 'He has the nerve to look me in the eye and tell me that, and I have patients on my list who have taken the medicine with no effect at all.'

I asked, 'Is the medicine no good, then?'

'Oh, no; it's really quite competent for immediate symptomatic relief. No cure, of course; there is no cure for asthma because it is caused by so many things, including psychosomatic problems.'

I said, 'What would you have wanted that salesman to say?'

'If he had said to me, "Doctor Black, it seems from extensive double-blind tests that this drug gives significant relief in almost eight out of ten severe asthma attacks," I would have asked to see the results of the tests and would have increased my prescribing rate for that drug. Damn it all, it's a good product, so why did he have to oversell it to me?'

One more example of just how idiotic (and unnecessary) it is to overclaim. We had a copying system which produced an extremely high-grade copy from a master sheet. It was ideal for a limited run of something where you wanted to impress the recipient. In normal conditions you could get twenty-five to thirty copies from one master, but we had decided to play it safe and guarantee twenty-five copies.

Now, our good salesmen would say something like this: 'We stand behind this master for twenty-five copies. If you have a delicate touch with the heat control on the machine, you might get a few more copies, but don't rely on it; count on twenty-five.' Fine; the customer got his twenty-five copies and occasionally got as many as thirty, whereupon he thought he was very clever and was delighted with the product.

Our 'smart' salespeople would say something like this: 'This is a terrific product; why, I get thirty or more copies from one master.' So the customer buys and gets anything from twenty-five to thirty copies. Now, notice something; he has managed to get exactly the same performance from the product that the first customer had got, but the first customer was happy and the second was angry. The difference? In the first case he was told the truth about the product, and in the second he was conned by our overclaimer.

The third rule then, that we never break unless we are begging for grief is: *never overclaim.*

The fourth complaint of the buyers was:

'He calls too often'

Well, we advanced salespeople have been saying that for years, but no, they all knew better than we did on this important point. We told our sales managers dozens of times that too frequent calling simply puts the customer off us, the products and the company. If he sees us coming in to call on him every time he raises his head, his reaction is going to be, 'Oh, God no; not again!'

And what about the first complaint we examined, about wasting the customer's time? Calling too often is a great way to waste the customer's time. But our sales managers just went on insisting that we keep on calling when we, as salespeople, knew that the call frequency was too high. Well, it seems that we were right all along!

Perfectly right, of course. Call too often on a customer and it begins to look to him as if he is the only person on our list and perhaps the only person in the world who is buying from us. Call too often and we can get into the tired old rut of: 'Hullo, Mr Parkington; I was just passing and I thought I would drop in and see if you needed anything.' This is, of course, one of the most common openings of a sales call, and it

[144]

also happens to be the worst thing we could possibly say. On the face of it, there seems little wrong with it; it seems to be a pleasant and friendly way to start. It is awful, because to the listener it can mean two things: first, it can sound as though we are saying: 'You aren't worth a special trip and I am only calling because I was passing anyway.' That is not good, but this translation is even worse: 'I actually don't seem to have anything to do today, and I thought that if you didn't have anything to do either, we could do it together.' Horrible. A salesperson should never appear to have nothing to do. We have already said that people like to deal with busy, successful people; not so busy that they can't give them the time that they need, but much too busy to hang around wasting people's time.

So, making sure we don't call too often is a rule we don't break. However, before you rush off and wave this chapter under the nose of your sales manager to prove to him that he has been making you call too often on your customers, please understand that this complaint came from thirty-five per cent of the buyers interviewed – a shade over one in three and quite a good proportion. What may shake you as it did me was that forty-seven per cent – nearly half – of the buyers had a diametrically opposed complaint:

'He doesn't call often enough'

And how do you like that, ladies and gentlemen? Better not show *that* to your manager or you will never hear the end of it; it is something that he has been saying for as long as you have been saying the opposite.

At first sight here our reaction could well be, what's the matter with these buyers and will they please make up their minds? Calling too often, not calling often enough – it has to be one or the other. If they can't get together on a simple thing like call frequency, then obviously the whole survey is suspect, so let's chuck this chapter in the shredder and go on to something more reliable.

In fact there is no contradiction here. A question to the research people elicited the fact that some of the buyers had actually given *both* answers – they said salespeople called too often and did not call often enough. What's all this about? The answer is simple and, I'm afraid, the problem is ours. The salespeople being talked about here have not worked out the optimum call frequency for their customers, so they are calling too often on some of them and not often enough on others.

You will clearly recognise the difference between 'optimum call frequency' and 'maximum call frequency'; the latter is over-calling, the former is the most *effective* number of calls which should be made, and we should know what that is for each one of our customers.

What should this be? Who knows? A potential customer for a power station or an oil tanker might be called on three times a year – and you might spend two weeks on the call. When we were monitoring the test-marketing of a fast-moving consumable through a chain-store we would call three times a *day*, and we would stay about five minutes.

Optimum Call Frequency is not a theoretical concept, to be discussed only in conference rooms during high-level seminars; it is a vital part of every salesperson's day-to-day job. I don't lean too much on my new trainees on this subject, they have plenty on their plates as it is. But you advanced salespeople should be using it to make the best possible use of your time and to extract the best possible potential from your customer.

How do you find the OCF for each customer? From three sources. First, your own knowledge and experience of the type of product you sell, the type of customer you call on, the type of territory you work in, the time of year if your product is seasonal, your customer's customers – all that sort of thing.

Second, your manager. Show him that you recognise the importance of calling not too often, not too seldom, and enlist his help.

Third, the customer himself. Show him that you don't intend to waste a second of his time, but that you intend to call as often as necessary to give him the prompt, personal service he deserves. Whether the call takes five minutes or five days – I'm quite serious, it can – you will be there when he needs you.

Do this and you will never break the golden rule which says *Call exactly as often as it takes – no more, no less.*

The next complaint, and what an interesting one it is, was:

'He doesn't come to me first'

Here the buyer is complaining about those salespeople who bypass his office and go directly to the people who use the products – the project engineer, the systems analyst, the works foreman, the journeyman, the office manager. There are two reasons for this complaint, one which you will hear from the buyer and one which you will not. The reason he gives (and it has merit, surely) is that when salespeople come into the company and wander around seeing all and sundry without first seeing the buyer, it can cause a fearful mess, with two people requesting similar products, with too much of one product and not enough of another being requisitioned, all of which makes the buyer's job more difficult than it already is. The reason you don't hear, and it could be the most important one to the buyer, is the simple and innocent one sometimes known as ALANO – Always Look After Number One. When you bypass the buyer and call on other people in his company, you are making his job smaller and less important, and while he has strength he will resist that with his last breath. It is a very human, natural and logical precept, and we have to recognise that it exists.

This chapter is called The Rules We Never Break. It is just possible, however, that the rule which says 'Always call on the buyer first,' can very occasionally be broken. We must tread warily here, and we certainly don't break this one as a way of life. But strong diseases need strong medicines, and yes, sometimes *as a last resort*, we may have to bypass the buyer. You will realise from your long dealings with that interesting sub-species, the buyer, that it really *is* a last resort, since in the process of bypassing him, which is nothing more or less than going behind his back, you stand a very good chance of antagonising him permanently, and you have to ask yourself if you can afford to make an enemy as powerful as that.

A salesperson put it this way: 'If I have been trying to get my product into a company for months and months by doing it the conventional way and seeing the buyer, and not only have I not got an order but I feel that I haven't made an inch of progress then yes, damn right I'll bypass the buyer. What have I got to lose?' In this case the product was a line of men's toiletries which the buyer for some reason had turned his back on; he simply wasn't interested. The salesperson knew that the shop in question was an ideal outlet for the product range, and she went to the manager of the men's department and spread the range out in front of him. The manager was most impressed and after a little discussion said, 'Fine; tell our buyer that we'll accept your recommended selection up to a value of £1,200.'

It was explained to him that, under the circumstances, this was not as easy as all that. He understood immediately, probably because he had already had similar problems with his buyer. He said, 'All right, leave it to me.' Three days later the salesperson got an order for the amount agreed on, to her selection, signed by the buyer. At the bottom of the order was the icy cold instruction: *do not call*. She was much too intelligent ever to ask what lever the manager had used on the buyer, and although she did call on the manager she was careful never to let the buyer see her on the premises. She had got the business by making an enemy. I have heard of a salesman being phoned by a buyer and told: 'The order which you gained through unethical behaviour is in the post. Don't ever call on me again.' The 'unethical behaviour' was bypassing the buyer.

What we are talking about here is 'Timbuctoo or bust' stuff, as I am sure you recognise. On very rare occasions I have bypassed a buyer myself, some turning out well, some disastrously. It is a last-ditch policy, and this is why it is in the 'We don't break it' chapter rather than in the 'Why not break it?' part of the book.

The next complaint, and it is enough to freeze the blood in your veins, is:

'He misses appointments!'

Here we have what every salesperson wants: a firm appointment with a potential customer who is expecting him at a fixed time, who is prepared to listen to his presentation and who (we can confidently assume) can afford to buy the product and has a use for it, otherwise he would hardly agree to the appointment in the first place. If the salesperson is experienced, with many such appointments behind him, he has a good idea of his strike rate and his chance of making a sale. Wonderful.

So he simply doesn't turn up for the appointment.

Why doesn't he just slash his wrists? What on earth could have possessed him to do a suicidal thing like that? You wouldn't think that it could happen often enough for buyers to complain about it, but there it was, high on their list of why they hated us salespeople.

Do I need to insist that the rule which says *don't ever miss appointments* is one we never break under any circumstances whatever? What? Oh, all right; personal, family emergencies always take precedence over any business situation. If your first-born gets rushed to the hospital with a burst appendix, then your whole world shrinks to that one terrifying fact, and you can make your apologies later. That, yes, but nothing else.

And I know what is in your mind because I have been there too. Here's the scenario: you have a series of appointments for a particular day, and as so often happens, you are slowly but surely falling behind. None of it is your fault; this one was delayed because you had to wait for the prospect's partner to come out of a meeting, that one took ten minutes longer than it should have, the other one had to be paged to come out of the archives and he didn't hear. You know exactly how it goes.

Anyway, it has now got to the stage where you are in the middle of a meeting with a customer and a quick look at your watch tells you that you are not going to get to your next appointment in time even if you go by surface-to-surface missile. Are you going to be one of those characters the buyers complained about, who makes appointments and then misses them?

Absolutely not. 'Mr Trent, we are right in the middle of something important here and I don't want to skimp on it. May I ask your secretary to phone my next call and ask if I may be thirty minutes late, or if that doesn't suit them, that I'll be at their service any time tomorrow afternoon? Thank you.'

[149]

The people who are expecting you are in business, too, and they have been in the same situation that you now find yourself, and as long as you let them know and don't leave them hanging, no blood will have been spilt. If you have ever done anything like this, you will probably have found as I have that the customer is gratified and impressed that you had the good manners to get someone to call them; it is, after all, what a true professional would do.

Unlike the salesman who practically fell on his knees with gratitude on the phone when I reluctantly agreed to see him at nine-thirty the following day. I say reluctantly, because I knew what he sold and I was not really in the market for it. The trouble is that I am still suffering from a vow that I made many years ago when, as a cub salesman, I was time and again refused an audience by uninterested people. I swore then that I would never refuse to give a salesman a hearing if he really wanted it, and so far I never have.

Well, nine-thirty came and went and no salesman. He finally turned up at nearly eleven, and it was clear that he was not in the best of moods. He slumped into a chair and immediately started talking about his product. When I interrupted to point out that he was grossly late for our appointment, he nodded grumpily. 'You're telling me,' he said. 'Would you believe it, I had a puncture and my spare was flat!' He glared at me as though it was somehow my fault. 'Anyway, let's get on,' he said. 'This business has ruined my schedule for the whole day.'

I said, 'Apparently I haven't made it clear that I have no more time for you. I have been waiting for you for nearly an hour and a half, and now my schedule also has been ruined.'

His mouth fell open. 'But I've explained that it wasn't my fault!'

I said, 'A telephone call would have taken you two minutes and saved me over an hour. I have no time for you, now or in the future.'

That was a missed appointment. A call from him would have allowed me to reschedule my morning and I would have been pleased to give him time the following day, probably commiserating with him about the way in which you always have a puncture when the spare is flat.

[150]

This book is concerned with the rules which we, as advanced salespeople, can and sometimes must break in order to win where, by sticking rigidly to those rules, we would never stand a chance. However, nothing in this book should ever allow us to forget that there are rules which we must *never* break. A pilot *never* takes off without checking the magneto drop. A doctor *never* gives an emetic for a corrosive poison. A chemist *never* adds water to acid, always acid to water.

There are rules which we can break when we have become proficient in using them, but there will always be the rules we *never* break.

Chapter 23

CUSTOMERS BREAK RULES, TOO!

While doing the research necessary to write this book, going through records of sales made and lost, I realised that a few instances were coming to light that didn't fit into any of the sections we have examined so far. In these instances rules were being broken, but not by salespeople; these were rules being broken by the *customers*.

Well, I thought, that's interesting, even though they have no part in the book. But, going deeper into the examples, I saw that we should indeed look at them, because they could give us a completely new slant on why people buy – or don't buy.

The main rule buyers break, and it is the one which we shall be examining here, goes like this: if there is a choice between two products, and there is no significant difference in specification or performance, buy the cheaper one. Kindergarten stuff, really; hardly worth mentioning. Pay more for a superior product, certainly, but if there isn't any worthwhile difference, then buy at the best price you can get.

I once benefited from a buyer breaking this rule. We had quoted a higher price than the opposition and the products were to all intents and purposes the same, and we were chosen. I have learnt not to question good fortune when she smiles on me and so I didn't rock the boat by asking the buyer why I had been the lucky one. Nevertheless, he told me. He said, 'Ever wonder why I picked you people for that order of control units when your price was higher and the units were about the same?'

I said, 'No, and quite frankly I didn't want to ask.'

He said, 'I bought yours in spite of the price disadvantage, because of the guarantee.'

I frowned. On the basis of 'Know your enemy' I had studied the opposition, and I knew that the terms of their guarantee were almost exactly the same as ours. I pointed this out to the buyer. He nodded grimly. 'Oh, yes, I know you both have the same non-conditional guarantee for twelve months and parts availability for five years. But a guarantee is only as good as the company which is backing it, and that other crowd is new in the industry and, from what I hear, is under-financed. I want my suppliers to be around when I claim on the guarantee.' He fixed me with a beady eye. 'You *will* be around when I have to dump on you, won't you?'

I said, not enthusiastically, 'Well, we've been around for twenty-three years, so I suppose we will.'

He grinned. 'That's my boy. That's why I accepted your exorbitant quotation.'

Good buying policy, made possible by breaking the rule, and not an uncommon practice with experienced buyers. Here the buyer had only one thing in mind when he made the decision, which was: what is in the best interests of the company?

The reason for this section is that buyers do *not* always have the best interests of their companies in mind, they break rules because of this, and we need to know why and how they do it. But please don't think that when I say they don't always have the company welfare and prosperity at heart, I am necessarily imputing anything unethical to the buyers. There are of course buyers who are in the job only for what they can get out of it; the bribes, the trips to the Bahamas, the perks. Forget those people, they are the lost souls. No, here we are looking at the normal, average person who has the authority to buy and whose honesty is not in question. Even this person can make a decision which is not in the interests of the company, sometimes without realising what he is doing.

The site foreman of a building company stubbornly stuck to his practice of buying a certain type of asbestos-cement piping, even though the new plastic pipe had obvious advantages over it. When I asked him why he continued doing what was, in fact, an old-fashioned job, he said curtly, 'It's the low-risk choice.' His manner barred any further discussion. I chewed over his explanation for some time; it simply didn't make sense. The plastic piping company stood behind their product one hundred per cent and if by any remote chance it had failed, it would have been replaced without question and all expenses would have been paid. What did the foreman mean?

What he meant, and it didn't dawn on me until much later, was that the old product, tried and tested as it was, was the low-risk choice – not for the building company but for the foreman. The asbestos-cement product worked, it did the job, and while he continued to use it he was not at risk. Try the new pipe and find that it didn't work and the site engineer might say to him, 'Made a bit of a bloomer there, Sid, didn't you? All right, chuck it back to the suppliers and stay with the stuff you know.' The foreman was thinking of his ego, not of the company, and so he broke a rule – that of getting the best product for the job within the limits of price, delivery and so on. He certainly didn't intend to ignore the company's interests; he would have been shocked and horrified if you had accused him of it. He was only looking after his job, as every single one of us does. Now, that sounds cynical, but it isn't really; our jobs are important to us and we will do things which will help us to retain them, enhance them or protect them, and if in the process we take decisions which are not in the best interests of our employers then so be it: ALANO.

Recognise this whenever a buying decision goes against you, when by any logical form of reasoning it should have come your way. Perhaps the buyer is breaking the rule which says, 'While thou art on thy company's time, thou shalt damn well have its best interests in thy mind.'

We can see the effects of this all the way through this book. If you go back through chapters such as Talk to the *wrong* people, Don't make friends with the customer, Be a show-off and others, you will see many examples of where the buyer was influenced by something of special interest and concern to himself rather than to his company.

I suppose the best way to wind up this short section is to make the point that when the curtain comes down, we are not selling to companies, farms, shops, hospitals, partnerships, committees, panels or groups but to *people*, and that they have all had much more experience at being people than they have at being buyers. Buyers break the rules, not because they are buyers, but because they are people, so let us never forget to sell to the *person* as well as to the *buyer* – they are both wearing the same pair of shoes.

Chapter 24
_____

LAST WORD. THE BASICS ARE IMPORTANT, BUT . . .

And that's about it. This list of rules we should break is not exhaustive and now that we have looked at them, you will be able to think of some more of your own. But let's go back to the first pages, where we talked about the basic rules of selling. I tried to make the point that before we can break them, we have to know them thoroughly; we have to be skilful in their use and completely familiar with them in every way. Nowhere in these pages have I implied that any salesperson can come out of his first-ever sales training course and leap into successful selling by breaking the basic rules he has just been taught.

I train people in the basics of the selling process – brand-new salespeople and mature and successful salespeople. Oh, yes; even advanced salespeople such as yourself sometimes need to be brought back into the training room and taken through the groundwork again. If your manager ever says, 'Hey, Bernard/Bernadette, you are going back to school next week for some sales training,' don't feel insulted; it is something we should all do – and regularly, too.

Do you remember the last time you flew? The pilot who took you up and brought you safely back to earth has many thousands of flying hours in his logbook, he is mature and experienced – but every year he goes back into the flight simulator and he is put through the absolute basics of his job. He has to know them backwards, forwards, sideways and up and down, and in the simulator they treat him just as though he was the newest recruit to the team. I know nothing about flying and I certainly don't want to know what rules, if any, the pilot will break when I fly again next week, but I do want to feel that he knows the basics.

When you do break the rules, you may find as I have done that the customer sits up and takes notice, perhaps for the first time since you have met him. On breaking a rule in selling, I have had customers say something like the following:

'Well, that's a new and refreshing approach.'

'I must say, I have never heard a saleman make a statement like that before; go on.'

'You must have a good reason for putting it like that, and I am not letting you out of this office until you have explained it to me.'

'Thirty seconds ago you were half an inch from being sent packing; now you have fifteen minutes of my time. Talk.'

'Well, I thought I had heard everything in selling, but I suppose you learn something new every day.'

Or even: 'You can't say that. Justify that statement or get out of here and don't come back.'

In spite of what the books and videos and trainers tell us, selling can turn into a humdrum round of calls; unexciting, mundane, *dull*. Break the rules in selling and find that your sales increase, your calls are interesting and your job is once more the exciting thing it always should be.

INDEX

The following books by Michael Beer may also be of interest. All Mercury books are available from booksellers or, in case of difficulty, from:

Mercury Books
862 Garratt Lane
London SW17 0NB
Tel: 081–682 3858

Further details and the complete catalogue of Mercury business books are also available from the above address.

DIARY OF A SALES MANAGER
Michael Beer

Diary of a Sales Manager is a year in the life of Tom Liskeard, Sales Manager of Hutton Horner. His successes and failures provide a wealth of lessons and pointers for anyone in sales management.

See how he –

- Handles the headaches of hiring staff.
- Organises the annual sales conference.
- Gets involved in the domestic problems of one of his team.
- Is head-hunted by a recruitment agency.
- Finds that sex raises its head in his office.
- Makes a mess of an incentive scheme.
- Realises that he is a husband and father as well as a sales manager.
- Is hit by a barrage of customer complaints.
- Discovers that Appraisal can be a powerful management tool.
- Deals with drunkenness at a convention.
- Has to give a bad reference to a departing salesperson.
- Faces the triumphs and disasters of any sales manager.

Diary of a Sales Manager is a highly informative manual for any present or aspiring manager.

£6.99 (paperback)   **ISBN 1–85252–048–5**

THE JOY OF SELLING
Michael Beer

Countless thousands of people have at one time or another considered entering the selling profession. They have been attracted by the idea of working with people, of dealing with fascinating products, of the interesting life-style of the modern salesperson – or simply by the potential for an income much higher than they enjoy now.

Unhappily, most of these people don't ever get into selling. There are too many questions which they need to ask and which nobody seems to be able to answer:

Could I really succeed in selling?

What sort of selling is best for me?

How do I go about getting a selling job?

And, after all that:

How do I learn to sell successfully?

You will find the answers to these questions (and dozens of others) in this book. Every detail is here to help you, from the moment you decide to go for it to the first time you sit down in front of a potential customer and make him yours.

Reading this book could be the most important step you have ever taken.

'There is a chronic shortage of good sales people – a shortage which has been getting steadily worse for many years. This book should make a major contribution to reducing this shortage and make thousands of people richer and happier.' John John Fenton

£5.99 (paperback)   ISBN 1–85252–024–8

LEAD TO SUCCEED
Michael Beer

When you are first promoted from the rank and file you can suddenly find yourself with a set of problems which you never had before and which you have no idea how to handle. These problems are almost all connected with *people*; managers find that they are expected to hire, train, supervise, motivate, discipline and sometimes fire the people on their team.

The problem is that the skills needed to achieve all this are not inherent or automatic; they must be learnt. Now, there are two ways of learning these skills. The first is by the seat of your pants, by slowly gaining experience on the job. The trouble with this method is that it is slow and it involves making mistakes along the way.

The second way is to watch others doing the job and to learn from their achievements – and from their mistakes. This way is what this book is all about. In these pages you will see how managers have handled the day-to-day people problems which cross every manager's desk. You will see the triumphs which they accomplish, and the disasters which they incur.

£5.99 (paperback)   ISBN 1–85252–032–9

THE JOY OF WINNING
Michael Beer

This is a completely different 'success' book. *The Joy of Winning* shows that to be a winner you don't have to be a superman – that you need no special aptitude, education, intelligence or character. You will learn that you can win without turning your life upside down; that you don't have to move mountains to be a winner. You may not even have to change your job!

Every chapter in *The Joy of Winning* is packed with ideas and information to help you become what you have always wanted to be in life, but have never known how to start. Just one idea from these pages could put you on the road to becoming a winner.

This book was written for ordinary people, who have always thought that winning was only for those with special talents and personalities. It shows you how to clear away the clutter that is stopping you from being what you want to be, and experience the joy of winning.

£5.99 (paperback)   ISBN 1–85252–081–7